VOLUME 24

CONVAIR B-36
"PEACEMAKER"

BY DENNIS R. JENKINS

specialtypress
PUBLISHERS AND WHOLESALERS

Published by
Specialty Press Publishers and Wholesalers
39966 Grand Avenue
North Branch, MN 55056
United States of America
(800) 895-4585 or (651) 277-1400
http://www.specialtypress.com

Distributed in the UK and Europe by
Midland Publishing
4 Watling Drive
Hinckley LE10 3EY, England
Tel: 01455 233 747 Fax: 01455 233 737
http://www.midlandcountiessuperstore.com

ISBN 1-58007-060-4

Printed in China

Front Cover: *A brand new B-36D-45-CF (44-92080) on the field at San Diego. This aircraft had originally been built as a B-36B-20-CF. The aircraft was redelivered to the Air Force in late 1951, but was written off on 29 January 1952 when it landed short at Fairchild AFB, killing seven crewmembers. (Convair via the San Diego Aerospace Museum)*
Back Cover (Left Top): *The first YB-60 prototype (49-2676). A close examination will reveal that the tail wheel is down, although it is mostly obscured by the main gear. Production aircraft would have had a longer and blunter nose that housed the APS-23 search radar and an APG-41 defensive systems radar. (Convair via the San Diego Aerospace Museum)*
Back Cover (Right Top): *Some of the damage from the tornado that hit Carswell AFB on 1 September 1952. This B-36D-15-CF (44-92077) and B-36H-5-CF (50-1096) were intertwined in an odd manner. The D-model sustained a fair amount of damage to the right horizontal stabilizer and the leading edge of the vertical stabilizer. Overall, 1 B-36D had been virtually destroyed and 82 others were damaged and 24 others were considered "seriously damaged." (U.S. Air Force via C. Roger Cripliver)*
Back Cover (Lower): *The lower aft turrets in their deployed configuration. The B-36 was the last U.S. bomber to carry a large defensive armament installation – sixteen 20-mm cannon in eight turrets. (U.S. Air Force)*
Title Page: *A B-36H-25-CF (51-5722) shows its open bomb bay doors and upper forward turret doors. The head for the Y-3 retractable periscopic bomb sight may be seen under the nose just behind the glazed panels. Note the white "high altitude camouflage" on the undersurfaces of the fuselage and wing. (Lockheed Martin)*

TABLE OF CONTENTS

CONVAIR B-36 "PEACEMAKER"

PREFACE

The story of the B-36 is unique in American aviation history. It survived near-cancellation on six separate occasions during an extremely protracted development program. It was the symbol of a bitter inter-service rivalry between the newly-formed Air Force and the well-established Navy over who would control the delivery of atomic weapons during the early years of the Cold War. The atomic mission also brought with it the lion's share of the funding and prestige, things both services wanted to keep largely for themselves. As a result of the bickering, the aircraft was the subject of numerous Congressional investigations and countless newspaper and magazine articles.

The B-36 served for only ten years, and there were always questions as to whether it could accomplish its assigned strategic bombardment mission. Nobody denied the aircraft was slow, although sometimes it was hard to ascertain just how slow it really was in comparison to other aircraft. Nobody advertised the weaknesses of their aircraft, and published performance figures were often misleading. However, the B-36 flew so high that it probably did not really matter, at least initially. Few fighters of its era could climb as high, and surface-to-air missiles were just being developed. It was probably not until the last few years of its service life that the B-36 was particularly vulnerable.

The aircraft also had very long legs, a necessary attribute for the first truly intercontinental bomber. It is hard to imagine a modern aircraft remaining airborne for two days without refueling, but it was not particularly unusual for the B-36 to do so. It took a long time to fly 10,000 miles at 250 mph.

Then there were the problems. The B-36, despite its seemingly obsolete appearance, pushed 1950s state-of-the-art further than any other aircraft of its era. Its sheer size brought structural challenges, while its high-altitude capabilities brought engine cooling and other problems. Sophisticated gun and bombing systems presented development, maintenance, and operational headaches. A lack of training for the ground crews, and severe spare parts shortages exacerbated the problems.

In the end, the B-36 did its job – for the first ten years of the Cold War, the

The XB-36 dwarfs a Boeing B-29 Superfortress, showing the sheer size required to achieve intercontinental range without in-flight refueling. (Convair via Don Pyeatt)

"Big Stick" carried by the B-36 was the major deterrent available to the Free World. The fact that we are here is a testimony to its effectiveness.

Curious about the quotation marks around the name "Peacemaker"? Convair had proposed the name for the B-36, but several groups opposed its adoption, and in the end the B-36 spent its entire career without an official moniker. "Peacemaker" is generally used, but was never officially sanctioned by the Air Force.

When the original edition of this book was written, there were not many books on the B-36. The most notable was by Meyers K. Jacobsen, who assembled six other authors to create *Convair B-36 – A Comprehensive History of America's "Big Stick"* published by Schiffer Military History, 1998. The book's 400 pages allowed the authors to go into significantly more detail on many subjects than was possible here. However, they also seemed to miss some things and continued several misconceptions. Nevertheless, anybody truly interested in the B-36 should look at a copy of Meyers' book.

However, during the writing of this monograph, I collected a great deal more material than could be used, much of it never before seen outside Convair. The popularity of this monograph convinced the publisher to produce a larger volume that allowed more detail to be covered. This resulted in Specialty Press releasing *Magnesium Overcast: The Story of the Convair B-36* during late 2001. If this monograph whets your appetite to learn more about the B-36, pick up a copy of *Magnesium Overcast* – there is more to the story.

No book can be produced in a vacuum and, more so than most, this one

A late-production Featherweight III B-36J leads its replacement (Boeing B-52 Stratofortress, lower center) and another famous Convair bomber, the supersonic B-58 Hustler in a formation flight on 30 May 1958. In February 1959, the last B-36 was retired, and SAC became an all-jet command. (Lockheed Martin)

is the product of tremendous cooperation from a great many people. As always, my good friends Peter M. Bowers, Walter J. Boyne, Frederick A. Johnsen, Tony Landis, Jay Miller, Terry Panopalis, and Mick Roth supplied information and photographs. Many B-36 enthusiasts also contributed from their personal collections. Don Pyeatt was first and foremost, going to great lengths to secure photos for me for the first edition of this monograph. Don went on to publish an excellent CD-ROM book on the restoration of the last B-36, but he continued to collect data and photos for me. He also put me in contact with many others: Max Campbell, Ed Calvert, Richard Freeman, Frank Kleinwechter, Richard Marmo, Wendell Montague, Bill Plumlee, George Savage, Joe Trnka, Bert Woods, and John W. "Zimmy" Zimmerman. All contributed greatly.

Photos and other material from the Jay Miller Collection in Little Rock are used courtesy of the Aerospace Education Center and the Central

Arkansas Library System. The assistance of Rob Seibert and others at the collection is greatly appreciated. This constantly growing Collection is becoming a truly world-class resource for aviation history researchers.

However, the unique content of this book is largely attributable to Mike Moore, Karen Hagar, and Diana Vargas at Lockheed Martin Aeronautics Company in Fort Worth (the former Convair). Mike spent many hours looking through the archives and uncovered things that everybody assumed were lost forever, if anybody knew the items existed in the first place. Several of the photos presented here have never been seen outside Convair. The efforts of Mike and his mentor, C. Roger Cripliver, are also responsible for much of the data that shed long-overdue light on many subjects covered herein.

Others who graciously contributed include: Bob Bradley (formerly of Convair, San Diego), Mark Cleary (45th SW/HO), Doug Davidge,

Dwayne A. Day, Scott Deaver, Robert F. Dorr, James Foss (P&W), Wesley Henry (Air Force Museum), Tom A. Heppenheimer, Teresa Vanden-Heuvel (AMARC Public Affairs), Ellen LeMond-Holman (Boeing St. Louis), Marty Isham, Colonel Doug Kirkpatrick (USAF, Ret.), Mike Lombardi (Boeing Historical Archives), MSgt. Gary T. McNeece (Fairchild Heritage Museum), David Menard, Claude S. Morse (AEDC/ACS), Major Bill Norton, Stan Piet, Greg W. Roberts (P&W), Frederick N. Stolik-er, Sheila Stupcenski (P&W), and Warren F. Thompson.

Ray Wagner and A.J. Lutz at the San Diego Aerospace Museum graciously allowed me access to their extensive photo archive – easily one of the best in the world when researching Convair subjects. My sincerest thanks go to Ed Lieser, also at the San Diego Aerospace Museum, who was largely responsible for getting me interested in aviation history in the first place.

Those interested in supporting one of the truly great collections of aviation history in this country should contact the:

San Diego Aerospace Museum
2001 Pan American Plaza
Balboa Park
San Diego, California 92101
(619) 234-8291.

Dennis R. Jenkins
Cape Canaveral, Florida
January 2002

"Development: DH-4 to B-36 of the Bomber" by John McCoy. The evolution of the bomber in the United States began with the De Havilland DH-4, although most of those in U.S. service were actually manufactured by Dayton-Wright or Fisher Body (General Motors). The DH-4 saw extensive use in World War I. Next is the Martin-Curtiss NBS-1, which equipped Army bombing squadrons during the mid-1920s. The NBS-1 used two of the same Liberty engine that the DH-4 had used a decade earlier. The first monoplane shown above is the Martin B-10, which began to enter service in the mid-1930s. It was quickly outclassed by the next aircraft shown – the famous Boeing B-17 Flying Fortress, which along with the Convair B-24 Liberator (not shown) saw extensive use during World War II. Boeing did not rest on its laurels, and by the end of the war had introduced the B-29 Superfortress, the product of one of the most amazing manufacturing programs ever undertaken. At the bottom of the illustration is the Convair B-36, the largest piston-engined bomber ever produced. (U.S. Air Force – DVIC photo DF-SC-84-08873)

DESPERATION

DEVELOPING A TRUE INTERCONTINENTAL BOMBER

The B-36 can trace its genesis to the early days of 1941, a time when it seemed that England might fall to a German invasion, leaving the United States without any bases outside the Western Hemisphere. It had taken Hitler just 20 days to crush the Polish army in September 1939, and but a few weeks for the German forces to speed across the Low Countries and France in 1940. Hitler's early successes against Russia would serve to underscore the concern. Consequently, the Army Air Corps (the Army Air Forces were not formally established until 20 June 1941) felt that it needed a truly intercontinental bomber, one that could bomb targets in Europe from bases in North America. To accomplish this, the Air Corps drafted requirements for a bomber with a 450-mph top speed, a 275-mph cruising speed, a service ceiling of 45,000 feet, and a maximum range of 12,000 miles at 25,000 feet with 10,000 pounds of bombs.[1]

(It should be noted that until the early 1950s, the range and speed of military aircraft were usually shown in statute miles. Afterwards, the Air Force began to measure speed in knots and range in nautical miles.)[2]

Requests for preliminary design studies were released to Consolidated and Boeing on 11 April 1941. The eventual winner of the design competition would receive $135,445 for the studies, while the losing bidder would get $435,623. Northrop was asked on 27 May 1941 to provide further information on its "flying wing," although the aircraft only had an 8,000 mile range with 2,000 pounds of bombs. Later, the Glenn L. Martin Company was also solicited but declined; work on the XB-33 and a Navy production contract were already stretching the company's engineering resources. Apparently, North American Aviation also toyed with designs to meet the specification, but was not formally involved in the competition.

Separately, Douglas was awarded a contract on 19 April 1941 to determine if the Allison V-3420 liquid-cooled engine could be used in a bomber. Douglas had also been working for several years on the XB-19, which had only recently flown and was the largest aircraft ever built in the United States. The Air Corps planned to use the XB-19 as a flying laboratory to gather information to assist in the design and construction of future very-large aircraft.

On 3 May 1941 preliminary design data was submitted by Consolidated under the company designation Model 35, with Boeing (Models 384 and 385) and Douglas also submitting preliminary data. The results were not encouraging. All of the manufacturers were having trouble designing an aircraft to meet the requirements. A conference was held on 19 August in an attempt to accelerate the bomber project, primarily by scaling back the specifications. This was a relative concept, and the revised requirements were still a tall order – a minimum range of 10,000 miles, and an effective combat radius

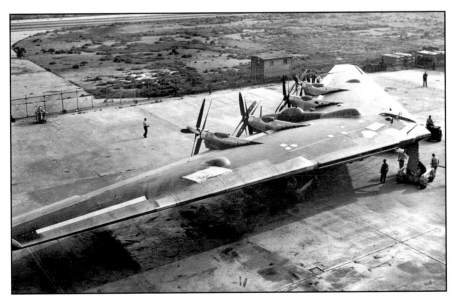

During the mid and late 1940s the Northrop flying wing designs were considered serious threats to the B-36 procurement. In the end, the B-35 (and later B-49 jet-powered versions) could not overcome several handicaps inherent in the flying wing design and were abandoned. It would be 30 years before Northrop finally built an operational flying wing – the B-2A Spirit. (Jay Miller Collection)

This is how Model 36 looked on 14 November 1941. Noteworthy are the characteristic Consolidated Vultee twin vertical stabilizers, the four-bladed propellers, and the lack of obvious gun turrets. Later versions of this design used a variety of manned gun turrets before the final remote-control units were adopted. (Convair via the San Diego Aerospace Museum)

of 4,000 miles with a 10,000-pound bomb load. This was four times the combat radius of the new B-17, and almost double that specified for the upcoming B-29. The requirements further specified that the bomber should have a cruising speed between 240 and 300 mph, and a 40,000-foot service ceiling. Each of the three contractors revised preliminary data to accommodate the new requirements, and all submitted proposals in early September 1941.

The Army Air Forces decided that the Consolidated proposal was the most promising. Douglas had stated that it did not desire to undertake an "out-and-out 10,000-mile airplane project," and proposed the development of the 6,000-mile range Model 423, which was rejected. The Boeing designs were "overly conservative" and the Army Air Forces believed that Boeing had not yet "really tackled the [long-range] airplane design with the necessary degree of enthusiasm." Given Boeing's preoccupation with B-17 production and B-29 development, this was understandable.

Brig. Gen. George C. Kenney, commander of the Experimental Division and Engineering School at Wright Field, Ohio, issued a recommendation to further pursue the Consolidated design. This was based on a detailed proposal that had been submitted on 6 October 1941 which asked for $15 million plus a fixed-fee of $800,000 for development, mock-up, tooling, and production of two experimental long-range bombers. Delivery of the first aircraft would take 30 months, and Consolidated stipulated that the project could not be "entangled with red tape" and constantly changing requirements.

On 15 November 1941 a contract (W535-ac-22352) was issued for two XB-36 experimental aircraft to be built at the Consolidated facility in San Diego. The first was to be delivered in May 1944 and the second six months later. Consolidated knew it would be faced with design prob-

A full-scale test nacelle was constructed for the P&W R-4360 engine and Curtiss-Wright 19-foot-diameter propeller. This allowed Convair to refine the installation and also gather acoustic and vibration data with the engine running. (Convair via C. Roger Cripliver)

lems that had not been previously encountered, mostly stemming from the aircraft's sheer size and operating altitude.[3]

Although the aircraft was generally similar to the original Model 35, there were sufficient differences for Consolidated to assign the aircraft a new model number – 36 – conveniently the same as the official designation. By this time, the wing span had grown to 230 feet with an area of 4,772 square feet, versus an original 162 feet and 2,700 square feet. The aircraft was to be powered by six 28-cylinder Pratt & Whitney "X-Wasp" air-cooled radial engines (which would become the R-4360 Wasp Major), each driving a 19-foot-diameter three-bladed Curtiss-Wright propeller in a pusher configuration. The engines were to be accessible for maintenance in flight through the wing, which was 7.5 feet thick at the root. In 1941 the new engine only existed on paper, although it was essentially two 14-cylinder R-1830 engines joined at the crankshaft.

Six fuel tanks with a capacity of 21,116 gallons were incorporated into the wing. The 163-foot long fuselage had four separate bomb bays with a maximum capacity of 42,000 pounds. The forward and aft crew compartments were pressurized and connected via a 25-inch diameter, 80-foot long pressurized tube through the bomb bays. Crewmen could use a wheeled trolley to slide back and forth. Four rest bunks, a small galley, and toilets were provided for the crew. Defensive armament was to consist of five 37-mm cannon and ten 0.50-caliber machine guns distributed between four retractable turrets (two on top of the fuselage, two on the bottom) and a tail turret.

The 10,000-mile range was a challenge, dictating that the aircraft would spend almost two days in the air. Every effort would have to be made to minimize the base drag of the aircraft, meaning particular attention would need to be paid to the aerodynamic smoothness of the skin and skin-joints. To emphasize the problem at hand, Consolidated constantly reminded engineers that for every pound of extra weight, it took two pounds of fuel to complete the 10,000-mile mission.

For six months Convair refined the design, exerting every effort to control weight, reduce drag, and elimi-

The partially-complete XB-36 is rolled out of the Experimental Building at Fort Worth. Note the open turret bay doors behind the cockpit, and the location of the open turret bay doors on the mid-fuselage. This configuration was unique to the XB-36, where the rear turret bay was located between bomb bay No. 3 and bomb bay No. 4 instead of behind the last bomb bay as on production models. Also note that the "island" in the forward turret bay is at the back of the bay instead of the front as it was on the B-36A and B-models. Only the XB-36 used the "stepped" canopy shown here – all later aircraft (except the NB-36H) used a "bubble" canopy. (Convair via the San Diego Aerospace Museum)

Looking much more complete, the XB-36 shows the massive 110-inch single main landing gear originally used for the undercarriage. The main landing gear doors have not yet been installed. (Convair via the Peter M. Bowers Collection)

nate the various developmental challenges typically encountered. The B-36 mockup was finally inspected on 20 July 1942, and weight estimates were much higher than expected. The Mockup Committee wanted to reduce the defensive armament and crew in order to meet the 10,000-mile range requirement. But some members argued that such changes would render the aircraft tactically useless and relegate it to much the same role as the XB-19 "flying laboratory." If a compromise could not be reached, many members believed that the entire project should be cancelled. The Mockup Committee eventually agreed to delete only "less neces-

sary" items of equipment such as some crew comfort and survival items, providing some weight reduction, and allowing the program to continue.

A month after the B-36 mockup inspection, Consolidated suggested shifting the XB-36 project from San Diego to its new government-leased plant in Fort Worth. The Air Force concurred that it made sense to move the development activity to the same facility that would eventually produce the airplane. The move was completed in September 1942, less than 30 days after being approved, but development was set back several months. Progress on

the B-36 was also slowed because of the higher priority of the B-24 Liberator, and later the B-32 Dominator.

Consolidated wanted the government to place a production order for the B-36, claiming that two years could be saved if preliminary work on production aircraft could be accomplished in parallel with the experimental models. However, the war in the Pacific was not going well, and the Army Air Forces felt that it should devote its full effort to aircraft which could contribute to the war effort sooner, so the request was denied.

Another Consolidated request in the summer of 1942 fared somewhat better. The Army Air Forces agreed to the development of a XC-99 cargo version of the XB-36, provided that one of the two experimental bombers was produced at least three months ahead of the cargo aircraft. Consolidated wanted the XC-99 to test the engines, landing gear, and flight characteristics of the forthcoming XB-36s. Consolidated also believed the XC-99 could be ready to fly much sooner than either of the XB-36s because armament and other military equipment was not required. Consolidated accepted the government's conditions and a $4.6 million contract was approved by year's end. See Chapter 2 for details on the XC-99 project.

On 17 March 1943, the Consolidated Aircraft Corporation merged with Vultee Aircraft, Inc., becoming the Consolidated Vultee Aircraft Corporation. This name was often truncated to "Convair," although this did not become official until 29 April 1954, when Consolidated Vultee Aircraft Corporation became the Convair division of the General Dynamics Corporation.[4] In between those years Con-

vair referred to itself alternately as CVAC, or CONVAIR (all caps).

While Consolidated wrestled with weight increases and various developmental troubles, world events suddenly boosted the importance of the B-36. By the spring of 1943, China appeared near collapse and neither the B-17 or B-24 had sufficient range to operate over the vast distances of the Pacific. The B-29 was in the early stage of production, but was proving to be troublesome in initial service. The parallel development of the B-32, generally considered by the Army Air Forces as "insurance" in case the B-29 failed, was not progressing as well as expected, largely because of a low priority rating in the national production scheme. Neither of these types could reach Japan from the continental United States, and extremely bloody battles would need to be won before the Mariana Islands could become bases for B-29 or B-32 operations. Speeding up B-36 development might provide a way for attacking the Japanese home islands directly.

The war in the Pacific dominated the discussion at the "Trident Conference" between President Roosevelt and Prime Minister Churchill in May 1943. After various consultations, Secretary of War Henry L. Stimson waived the customary procurement procedures and authorized the Army Air Forces to order the B-36 into production without waiting for the completion of the two experimental aircraft. A letter of intent for 100 B-36s was signed on 23 July, each with an estimated cost of $1,750,000, just slightly more than two days' cost of the war effort. Subsequently, the priority assigned to the B-36 program was raised, although still not to a level equal to the B-29, or even the B-32.

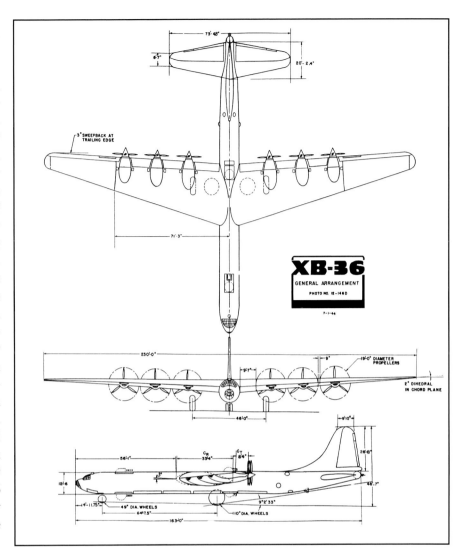

A July 1944 three-view drawing of the XB-36 shows the location of the four gun turrets. The lower forward turret would be deleted in production models to provide room for the search radar antenna, while the two aft turret locations would be moved rearward in back of bomb bay No. 4. (Convair)

Further evaluation led to the Model 36's original twin tail being deleted in favor of a single 47-foot-high vertical stabilizer. This would decrease weight by 3,850 pounds, provide additional directional stability, and lower base drag. It was also in keeping with the general direction of the aircraft industry at the time. Some of the initial designs for the B-29 had twin tails, but Boeing had selected a taller single unit for production. Even Consolidated had begun with twin verticals on the B-32, but the type ultimately used a single vertical surface (the PB4Y-2 variant of the B-24 also was produced with a single vertical, as were a few late-model B-24s). The modification was approved on 10 October 1943, along with a 120-day delay in delivery. At best the Army Air Forces would not get its first XB-36 until September 1944.

By mid-1944, the military situation in the Pacific had improved. The Marianas campaign was near its end, and preparation was being made to

The XB-36 on 19 February 1946. The trailing edges of the horizontal stabilizer and elevator had been previously fitted and installed, but were removed for test purposes. The opening in aft end of fuselage will be provided with an aerodynamic cone in lieu of the tail turret. The black objects on the vertical stabilizer are weights being used for loads verification. (Convair)

deploy B-29s from these bases to attack the Japanese home islands. The B-29's initial difficulties were mostly resolved, and the Army Air Forces believed that a very long-range bomber was no longer urgently needed. Nevertheless, on 19 August 1944, a $160 million contract (including a $6 million fixed fee) was finally signed to cover the production of 100 B-36s. The contract did not carry any priority rating at all, essentially ensuring that no parts or materials could be procured as long as the war lasted. Delivery schedules, however, were unchanged, and the first production B-36 was to be delivered in August 1945, with the last arriving in October 1946.

Following Germany's surrender and the end of the war in Europe, production contracts were drastically cut back. Aircraft production was cut by 30 percent on 25 May 1945, a reduction of 17,000 aircraft over an 18-month period.[5] However, the contract for the B-36 was untouched. The enormous losses suffered in seizing island bases in the Pacific confirmed that there was a need for a very long-range bomber. The atomic bomb, unlikely to remain an American monopoly, was another strategic justification. Since any U.S. retaliation would have to be quick, there would be no time for conquering faraway bases. And, realistically, a very-long-range bomber could be the best deterrent for the immediate future. From the economic standpoint, the B-36 also looked good. It out-performed the B-29 and the B-35 "flying wing" for long-range missions, and was cheaper by half to operate than the B-29 in terms of cost per ton per mile.

While the fate of the B-36 program vacillated with changing wartime priorities, the aircraft's development remained painfully slow. By 1945 Convair still worried over the weight of the R-4360-25 engine – Pratt & Whitney's third version of the proposed X-Wasp. Adding nose guns, a new requirement based on wartime experience, required an extensive rearrangement of the forward crew compartment that would become standard beginning with the second

aircraft. New radio and radar equipment would add at least 3,500 pounds, and potentially more if the antenna of the AN/APQ-7 bombing radar could not be installed in the leading edge of the wing. Coupled with a 2,304-pound increase for the engines, this presented a serious weight problem for the engineers.

Due to the sheer size of the aircraft, the landing gear presented its own set of problems. In order to fit the main gear into the wing when it was retracted, Convair decided to use a single 110-inch diameter tire per side. Unfortunately, this concentrated most of the aircraft's weight onto only two comparatively small contact patches, one on each side of the aircraft. Only three runways in the world were capable of withstanding the huge amount of stress this would impart when the aircraft landed and during taxi. (The three were Fort Worth, Eglin Field in Florida, and Fairfield-Suisun AAF – later Travis AFB – in California.) In addition to the runway restrictions, it put the entire aircraft at risk if a single tire failed at a critical time. The 110-inch Goodyear tires, each weighing 1,475 pounds, were the largest aircraft tire ever manufactured. Each tire had a 225-pound inner tube pressurized to 100 psi. The wheels weighed 850 pounds each, and the dual multiple-disk brakes on each wheel added 735 pounds. Complete with the struts and ancillary equipment, each main gear weighed 8,550 pounds.

In mid-1945 the Army Air Forces directed that a new landing gear be devised to distribute the aircraft weight more evenly, thus reducing the need for specially built runways. One of the major problems encountered with designing a multi-wheel undercarriage for the B-36 had been developing adequate brakes. These

The XB-36 made a 37-minute maiden flight on 8 August 1946 piloted by Beryl A. Erickson and G.S. "Gus" Green, assisted by seven other crewmembers. The large main wheels had not been fitted with their doors. At the time this was the largest and heaviest landplane ever flown. (Convair via the San Diego Aerospace Museum)

were finally available and the production four-wheel bogie-type undercarriage using 56-inch tires allowed the B-36 to use any airfield suitable for the B-29.

Revised estimates of the XB-36's performance were proving discouraging. Gross weight had increased from 265,000 to 278,000 pounds. Top speed had gone from an estimated

NEW RUNWAY UNDER CONSTRUCTION FOR B-36

The B-36 project necessitated a longer runway at the Fort Worth plant, a facility shared with Carswell AFB. This is the new runway being constructed in August 1945. The Convair plant is at the upper right; Carswell is off to the left. (Convair via C. Roger Cripliver)

The wheel wells on the XB-36 had to be large to accommodate the 110-inch tires. Note the scale of the workman. The hatch just behind him led into the fuselage, and it was possible to crawl into the wings during flight to perform minor maintenance on the engines or landing gear. (San Diego Aerospace Museum Collection)

369 to 323 mph, while the service ceiling had dropped from 40,000 to 38,200 feet. Although it was estimated that the B-36 might not be any faster than the B-29, it was still vastly superior in terms of range and payload. A single B-36 would cost three times as much as a B-29, but could carry 72,000 pounds of bombs half-way on an estimated 5,800 mile flight, while the B-29 could only carry 20,000 pounds of bombs a little over 2,900 miles. In terms of airframe weight, the B-36 was 1.85 times as heavy as the B-29, but it could carry over 10 times the bomb load to 5,500 miles.

Meanwhile, faulty workmanship and substandard materials were discovered in the XB-36. In fairness to Convair, substituting materials was a generally accepted practice during the war years, especially for experi-

The 110-inch main landing gear was a great deal taller than an average person. This is actually the XC-99 with its flight crew prior to its maiden flight. (Convair via the San Diego Aerospace Museum)

The size of the XB-36's vertical stabilizer is well illustrated here with two men standing next to it. By any measure the B-36 was a large aircraft, especially by 1946 standards. (Peter M. Bowers Collection)

mental aircraft. It was expected that the structural limitations would render the XB-36 useless, other than as a test vehicle for the initial flights.

Finally, on 8 September 1945, almost six years after the original letter contract had been signed, the XB-36 (42-13570) was rolled out. The aircraft made a 37-minute maiden flight on 8 August 1946 piloted by Beryl A. Erickson and G.S. "Gus" Green, assisted by seven other crewmembers. At the time, it was the largest and heaviest aircraft ever flown. Early test flights confirmed that the aircraft's top speed was only about 230 mph, and two major problems soon surfaced – a lack of proper engine cooling and propeller vibration, although both of these had been extensively investigated during wind tunnel testing. Eventually a two-speed cooling fan was developed that largely eliminated the cooling problem, but nothing could be done to ease the vibration other than strengthening the affected structures, which added yet more weight.

The XB-36 was flown for 160 hours by pilots from the Air Materiel Command before being returned to Convair where company pilots made 53 additional test flights, logging a total of 117 hours. The airframe was ultimately turned over to the Air Force in mid-1948, but as predicted, it had limited value and was used primarily for ground training.

The XB-36 did participate in one further test series. In early 1950, an experimental track-type landing gear was installed, similar to ones also tested on a C-82 and B-50 around the same time. The specially-designed Goodyear system of V-belts applied only 57 psi to the runway, compared to 156 psi for the production four-wheel bogie-type undercarriage.

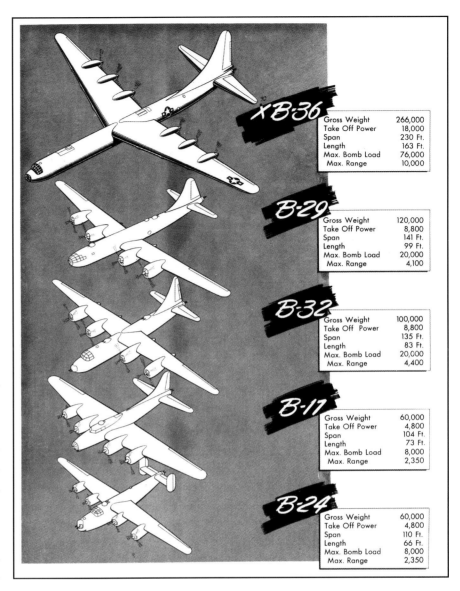

XB-36	
Gross Weight	266,000
Take Off Power	18,000
Span	230 Ft.
Length	163 Ft.
Max. Bomb Load	76,000
Max. Range	10,000

B-29	
Gross Weight	120,000
Take Off Power	8,800
Span	141 Ft.
Length	99 Ft.
Max. Bomb Load	20,000
Max. Range	4,100

B-32	
Gross Weight	100,000
Take Off Power	8,800
Span	135 Ft.
Length	83 Ft.
Max. Bomb Load	20,000
Max. Range	4,400

B-17	
Gross Weight	60,000
Take Off Power	4,800
Span	104 Ft.
Length	73 Ft.
Max. Bomb Load	8,000
Max. Range	2,350

B-24	
Gross Weight	60,000
Take Off Power	4,800
Span	110 Ft.
Length	66 Ft.
Max. Bomb Load	8,000
Max. Range	2,350

Early diagram developed to show the relative size and performance of the heavy bomber force. (San Diego Aerospace Museum Collection)

This would, in theory, allow very large aircraft to use unprepared landing strips. The first flight using the new landing gear came on 26 March 1950, and the resulting "screeching" sound was unnerving to those aboard the aircraft and nearby observers. There was never any intention of using the track-type gear on production B-36s, and the XB-36 was used as a testbed simply because it was a heavy aircraft that was available. There was, however, some consideration given to using it on production C-99 transports.

The XB-36 was not representative of later aircraft. In addition to the material deficiencies caused by its wartime construction, both the forward fuselage and the bomb bay configurations were different than the production specification. Because of this, the Air Force decided it would be too expensive to bring the XB-36 up to production standards. Subsequently, the aircraft was officially retired on 30 January 1952. The airframe was assigned to the atomic airplane program and was used for some engineering studies. In the end however,

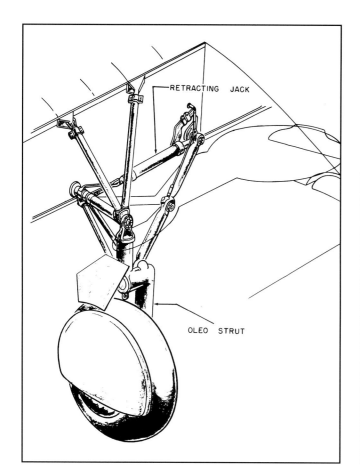

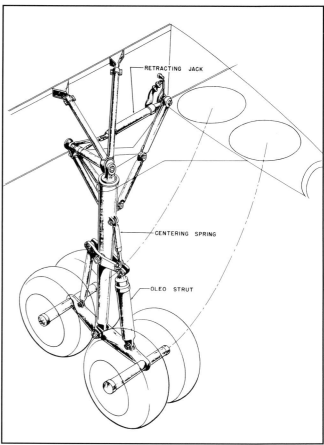

The four-wheel undercarriage used the same mounting locations as the original 110-inch gear. Unfortunately the bogie was thicker, necessitating a "bump" on top of the wing and "bulged" landing gear doors to accommodate the new wheels and tires. These bumps are clearly evident on any photo of later B-36s. Only the XB-36, YB-36, and XC-99 used the large 110-inch landing gear, and all were later fitted with the revised undercarriage. (Convair)

the engines and all serviceable equipment were removed, and the aircraft fell into disrepair in a corner of the Fort Worth field. In May 1957 the airframe was given to the Carswell AFB fire department to be used as a fire-fighting aid, and was eventually consumed by fire.

YB-36

A decision had been made on 27 April 1945 to finish the second XB-36 (42-13571) closer to the expected production standard. The aircraft was redesignated YB-36 and flew for the first time on 4 December 1947. It had the new raised flight deck and canopy, a redesigned forward crew compart-

ment, and provisions for a nose turret. The aft bomb bays and turret bays were also rearranged to the production standard. Having the aft two bomb bays next to each other allowed them to be combined to carry large bombs, much like the front bomb bays could be. However, the YB-36 still had the original single-wheel undercarriage, and lacked armament and most production equipment. During the YB-36's third flight, it reached an altitude of more than 40,000 feet, an outstanding achievement for the time.[6]

After 89 hours of flight testing, the YB-36 was grounded for modifications. The single-wheel landing gear was replaced by the production

bogie-type four-wheel undercarriage and 3,500 hp R-4360-41 engines were fitted. The aircraft first flew in this configuration in June 1948, and was turned over to the Air Force on 31 May 1949. The YB-36 was returned to Convair in October 1950 to be remanufactured into an RB-36E in lieu of the first B-36A. During early 1957 the aircraft was retired and turned over to the Air Force Museum at Wright-Patterson AFB, but it was scrapped when the new museum facility was built. Parts of the aircraft were acquired by Ralph Huffman for $760, or roughly 3/4 cent per pound. Huffman subsequently sold the remains to Walter Soplata, and they still exist on a farm in Newbury, Ohio.

A careful examination of this XB-36 photo will show that the main landing gear is still uncovered. Like all early B-36s, the XB-36 did not carry any defensive armament. Also note the lack of an APS-23 radome under the forward fuselage. (Convair via the Peter M. Bowers Collection)

STRATEGIC AIR COMMAND

The Strategic Air Command (SAC) had been established by the Army Air Forces on 21 March 1946, and on 12 December 1946 its commander, Gen. George S. Kenney, suggested that the contract for 100 production B-36s should be reduced to only a few service test aircraft. At the time Boeing was in the process of developing the B-50 (originally designated B-29D), which Kenney believed had superior performance. Among the shortcomings Kenney listed for the B-36 were an effective range of only 6,500 miles, insufficient speed, and a lack of armor for the crew and fuel.[7] (This was somewhat unfair since the underwing skin was a fairly thick 75ST aluminum alloy that

The XB-36 was eventually fitted with the revised undercarriage, shown here. Note the configuration of the bomb bays (Nos. 1, 2, and 4 shown open in the photo) – the aft lower turret bay is located between bomb bay No. 3 (behind the main landing gear) and bomb bay No. 4 (between the propellers and the national insignia). This configuration was unique to the XB-36 and would change on production aircraft. The "buzz" number adorned the forward fuselage of most Air Force aircraft in the late 1940s and early 1950s. The "BM" indicated the type of aircraft, while the "570" was the last three digits of the serial number. (Peter M. Bowers Collection)

The unique tracked landing gear that was tested on the XB-36, as well as a B-50 and C-82 around the same time. The main tracks (below left) and nose tracks (below right) would have allowed landing on relatively unprepared fields. (Lockheed Martin)

The YB-36 shows the new nose profile, complete with a trials nose turret, but the aircraft still has the original 110-inch landing gear. This too would soon be replaced by production units. Note that the large search radar radome is installed in what was originally the lower forward turret bay. (Lockheed Martin)

was resistant[8] to 0.50-caliber rounds striking from most angles, and production aircraft were equipped with armored engine cowlings[9] and removable "bullet sealing pads" under the wings to further protect the fuel and oil tanks.)

However, neither the Air Staff nor Lt. Gen. Nathan F. Twining, the commander of the Air Materiel Command, agreed with this assessment. They felt that the problems being experienced by the B-36 were normal for the stage of development and could be solved given sufficient time. Besides, the B-50 could not fly as far as the B-36 without resorting in-flight refueling, and was not much faster. In any case, the B-36 was the only long-range bomber that was capable of carrying the full range of nuclear weapons in the arsenal, many of which were too large for smaller aircraft like the B-50. Gen. Carl Spaatz, the commander of the Army Air Forces, agreed with Twining, and the B-36 contract was retained.

On 6 January 1947, the results of a planning exercise for a global flight by a B-36 was published by Con-vair.

The clean shape of the original XB-36 was the result of careful design to minimize drag and increase range. (Convair via Don Pyeatt)

The aircraft would be extensively modified – all armament would be removed; all antennas and radomes would be removed and faired over; the sighting blisters would be faired over; the bombardier, radar operator, and all gunners seats, instrument panels, and other equipment would be removed; the bunks and galleys would be replaced by lighter weight versions; and even the forward crew compartment carpeting would be deleted. In all, this would save over 5,000 pounds. Six new flexible fuel cells would be installed in the wings, along with four bomb bay fuel tanks. Bomb bay No. 4 would also include provisions for four Aerojet 4,000 pounds-thrust JATO bottles to be used during takeoff.[10]

The XB-36 nose profile was more streamlined than the final production nose, but lacked a nose turret, something that had proven valuable during combat. Note the tracked landing gear. (Convair)

Convair built a wooden mockup of the revised nose section to work out the details of the equipment and turret installation. Compare with the original nose profile of the XB-36 shown at left. (Convair via the San Diego Aerospace Museum)

The modified aircraft would have a range of 15,075 miles at an average cruising speed of 210 mph. The proposed route used Idlewild Airport, New York, as the departure point, following a great circle route over Scotland, Berlin, the Black Sea, Southern Russia, Tokyo, the Aleutian Islands, Vancouver Island, and finally landing at Fort Worth. If favorable winds were encountered, a landing back at Idlewild would be attempted. The fact that part of the flight was over Russia, by a strategic bomber, did not seem to deter the planners. As far as is known, perhaps fortunately, the flight never took place.

The Air Force was established on 26 July 1947, when the National Security Act of 1947 became law. It began functioning as a separate service on 18 September 1947.

POWERFUL ENGINES

The Pratt & Whitney R-4360 Wasp Major engine was used to power the B-36, B/KB-50, C/KC-97, C-119, and C-124 aircraft. It represents the most technically advanced and complex reciprocating aircraft engine produced in large numbers in the United States. The passing of the KC-97 from the Air Force inventory in the late 1970s marked the closing of the era of both the large piston and turbo-supercharger within the Air Force.

The R-4360 was a 28-cylinder, 4-row radial, air-cooled engine with a gear-driven supercharger and two exhaust-driven turbo-superchargers. As the name suggests, the engine displaced 4,360 cubic inches (71.5 liters), and each cylinder had a 5.75-inch bore and 6.00-inch stroke (155.7 cubic inches per cylinder). The engine had a compression ratio of 6.7:1 in most applications. The R-4360 was 96.5 inches long, with a diameter of 55.0 inches. At maximum rpm, each piston was covering 2,700 feet per minute. The engine weighed 3,670 pounds (the weight and dimensions are for the basic engine only, without the turbochargers or reduction gears). The engine used 2,500 pounds of 115/145-grade aviation fuel and 25,000 pounds of air per hour at maximum output.[11]

The engine was rated at 3,500 hp (3,000 in early –25 engines; 3,800 in very late –53 units), but what is frequently overlooked was its torque rating. At 1,000 rpm, each engine provided 840 pound-feet of torque – by 3,000 rpm this had increased to a

Several different configurations were tried for the XB-36 nose landing gear. The gear shown (on 24 May 1946) has independent rotating wheels. This was replaced on 28 May with co-rotating wheels. The later configuration was adopted for production. (Convair via the San Diego Aerospace Museum Collection)

staggering 7,506 pound-feet, measured at the crankshaft. Because of the gearing selected, this was increased to over 20,000 pound-feet at the propeller shaft.

At 20,000 feet, without the use of turbo-supercharging, the R-4360-41 would have had an output of only 1,000-hp; with its use the power output improved to 3,500 hp. The R-4360 used two different supercharging techniques. An "internal supercharger" was mounted in the airstream immediately behind the carburetor and before the cylinders. This impeller was driven by the crankshaft by a gear train at a fixed ratio. At takeoff the impeller was turning at 17,000 rpm, with a tip speed of nearly 700 mph. The use of this supercharger was somewhat of a trade-off, for although it provided a doubling of the intake pressure (from 30 inches to over 60 inches), it also added a lot of heat to the intake charge, which is generally undesirable. It was felt that the benefits outweighed the drawbacks. Interestingly, it took 435 hp to drive the supercharger. It was worth it – the supercharger increased the power output by a staggering 1,930 hp.

Each engine was also provided with two General Electric Model B-1 exhaust-driven turbo-superchargers arranged in parallel. The primary purpose of the turbos was not to increase the power rating of the engine. Instead, they allowed the sea-level power rating to be maintained up to 35,000 feet, with a gradual degradation at altitudes above that. At sea level, the turbos had the theoretical ability to provide 300 inches of manifold pressure – obviously something that could not be allowed to happen. Automatic controls kept the turbos from overcharging the system at

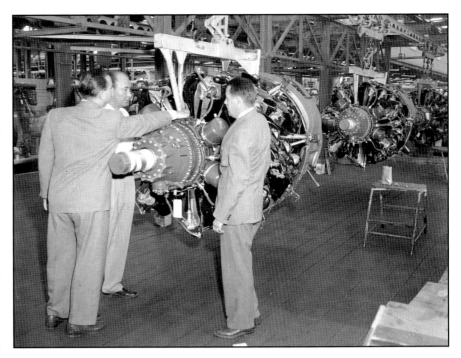

R-4360 engines freshly delivered from Pratt & Whitney awaiting installation at Convair. Convair used this area to add accessories to the engines prior to them being covered by their nacelles and installed on the aircraft. (Lockheed Martin)

any given altitude. Each turbocharger was equipped with an intercooler to remove waste heat from the air.[12]

Heat rejection was a major concern with an engine as powerful as the R-4360. The design of the cylinders and the use of forged aluminum

A cut-away R-4360 being prepared for display with the Fort Worth B-36J. Note the four rows of cylinders, and the supercharger on the left side of the photo. (Aviation Heritage Association via Don Pyeatt)

The flight deck of the XB-36 was decidedly different than later aircraft. Note the glazed bombardier's nose forward of the two pilots. (Convair via the San Diego Aerospace Museum)

alloy for the heads and barrel muffs permitted the machining of closely-spaced deep fins that provided a 30 percent increase in exposed fin area over that previously available from cast heads. Cooling air was inducted at the leading edge of the wing and was boosted by a large engine cooling fan before being routed by a series of baffles around the engine. Control over the amount of cooling air admitted to the nacelle was controlled by positioning an "air plug" located between the trailing edge of the nacelle and the propeller. These air plugs performed the same function as the cowl flaps on tractor installations.[13]

Even the Curtiss-Wright constant-speed, full-feathering, reversible propellers on the B-36 were unique. Their sheer size, and the fast rate-of-pitch change required, eliminated the possibility of using the traditional electric motor to control the variable pitch. Instead the designers developed a system that used the part of the power being transmitted via the propeller shaft. Pitch change was accomplished by transmitting power taken from the rotating propeller shaft through a series of gears and four clutch mechanisms. Hydraulic pressure was generated by a self-contained oil pump, and used by either the clutch or the brake on each blade, as directed via electrical control signals from the cockpit. Engine exhaust was directed through the propeller hub to the hollow blades to prevent ice buildup.

[1] Marcelle Size Knack, *Post-World War II Bombers*, Office of Air Force History, 1988, p 3. [2] *Ibid*, p 5. [3] *Ibid*, p 7. [4] *Ibid*, p 5. [5] *Ibid*, p 11. [6] *Ibid*, p 19. [7] Aviation Week, 15 August 1949, p 13. [8] Aviation Week, 18 October 1948, p 13. [9] Convair report FZA-36-061, *Preliminary Proposal for Global Flight of the B-36 Airplane*, 6 January 1947. [10] *Ibid*. [11] SAC Manual 50-35, *Aircraft Performance Engineer's Manual for B-36 Aircraft Engine Operation*, 1953. [12] AN 01-5EUC-2 (1B-36D-2), *Erection and Maintenance Instructions, USAF Series B-36D Aircraft*, 3 June 1954. [13] SAC Manual 50-35.

As early as May 1942 Consolidated had investigated a cargo variant of the XB-36 that used the bomber's wing, tail, engines, and landing gear. The Army Air Forces finally ordered a single example (43-52436) on 31 December 1942 under a $4.6 million contract (W535-ac-34454) that specified the XC-99 project was not to interfere with the construction of delivery of the XB-36.[1] Interestingly, the fact that an entire new fuselage needed to be designed was not considered to be high risk, and Convair viewed the XC-99 as an easy and expeditious way of verifying several aspects of the B-36 design since no military equipment needed to be provided for the aircraft. The XC-99 would prove to be the largest piston-engine cargo aircraft ever developed.

The Model 37 which was eventually built as the XC-99 could carry over 100,000 pounds of cargo, 400 fully-equipped troops, or 300 litter patients. Total cargo volume was 16,000 cubic feet split between two decks. The aircraft's range was estimated to be 1,720 miles with a 100,000-pound load, or 8,100 miles with 10,000 pounds. Cruising speed was 292 mph, with a top speed of 335 mph at 30,000 feet. The fuselage was 20 feet high, 14 feet wide, and 182.5 feet long, and mockups were constructed at San Diego to optimize the cargo loading and unloading concepts. Eight crewmembers were required to operate the aircraft: pilot, copilot, two flight engineers, navigator, radio operator, and two scanners. The scanners were stationed on the lower deck in the aft section near windows to observe the operation of the engines and landing gear. The scanners doubled as cargomasters while the aircraft was on the ground.[2] The flight deck was carpeted and soundproofed, and black fluorescent lighting was provided at all crew stations for night flying.[3]

The aircraft had a design gross weight of 265,000 pounds, but the operating manual allowed an "over-condition" weight of 295,000 pounds with "favorable atmospheric conditions when operating from known runways." This allowed 117,000 pounds of cargo to be carried, and still permitted a normal 500-feet-per-minute rate of climb at sea level. Initially the aircraft was equipped with over 12,000 pounds of flight test instrumentation that provided detailed information on control movements and forces, engine and duct temperatures, duct velocities, and valve movements in the various systems.[4] In late 1950, the same landing gear modifications made to the B-36 fleet were incorporated, allowing a gross weight of 357,000 pounds.[5]

The XC-99 used the B-36's wings, engines, landing gear, horizontal stabilizer, rudder, and structural portions of the vertical stabilizer with a new wide-body fuselage. The goal was to create a testbed for B-36 systems that could also lead to future production as a cargo transport. Although the resultant aircraft provided valuable service for almost ten years, no others were ever manufactured. Here a B-36A (44-92013) is shown at San Diego while the XC-99 is being overhauled. (Convair via the San Diego Aerospace Museum)

The XC-99 used a unique flight deck arrangement. Most of the controls and instruments were placed such that the flight engineer did not need a dedicated station, and was seated at the rear of the large center console (the back of his seat can be seen in the lower center). Russell R. Rogers (Chief of Flight Test at San Diego) is on the right, and Roberts R. Hoover (XC-99 Project Engineer) is on the left. (Convair via the Peter M. Bowers Collection)

The airframe weighed 135,232 pounds: fuselage 25,164 pounds, wings 37,100, empennage 4,659, landing gear 18,738, engines and nacelles 42,345, and miscellaneous equipment 7,226. Aluminum and magnesium alloy accounted for 75,000 pounds, steel for 18,000, and glass for 2,000. The remainder was made up of rubber, plastic, fabric, and other metal alloys.[6]

To achieve maximum safety for crewmembers and passengers, Convair located the inboard fuel tanks some 10 feet outboard from the fuselage. A supplemental bulkhead between the inboard fuel tank and the fuselage served as a secondary dam in the event of fuel leakage and prevented entry of fuel into the fuselage, minimizing the fire hazard inherent with fuel tanks located in

the fuselage area.[7] This essentially reduced the fuel capacity of the aircraft slightly from that carried by the B-36 since the smaller auxiliary fuel tanks normally located in the inboard section of the wing were deleted.

Even during the war Consolidated pitched a commercial version[8] of the aircraft to several airlines. Pan American World Airways ordered 15 of

the aircraft in February 1945, and production of the "Super Clippers" would begin as soon as the war ended. Each of the airliners could carry 204 passengers and 15,300 pounds of baggage and mail. Six 5,000-hp turboprop engines would be used, driving 19-foot three-bladed propellers. The interior arrangement featured a mixture of dayplane seats and sleeper berths, with spacious lounges located on each of the two decks, and large circular staircases located on each end of the aircraft. A full galley would offer gourmet meals, and the lavatory facilities resembled a fine hotel more than a modern airliner. But it was not to be, and the "wide body" era would have to wait another 20 years until the Boeing 747 was introduced.

Pan Am also asked Convair to investigate a flying boat derivative of the huge aircraft.[9] The basic design of the aircraft was similar, except the six turboprop engines drove counter-rotating three-bladed 16-foot-diameter tractor propellers instead of the larger pushers. And of course the fuselage incorporated a hull design. The elimination of the landing gear and its supporting structure allowed a weight savings of 6,500 pounds, even after the modified hull and retractable wing floats were added. But the additional drag generated by the hull and floats meant the flying boat would need to carry 3,000 pounds more fuel to achieve the same nominal range. Nevertheless,

this meant the flying boat could, in theory, carry 3,000 pounds more cargo. The design had a range of 4,200 miles at 25,000 feet and 332 mph – 10 mph slower than the conventional aircraft. Its maximum service ceiling was reduced from 30,000 feet to 29,100, and its takeoff distance increased from 4,760 feet (for the landplane) to 5,680 feet. It would take 48 seconds for the flying boat to clear the water after it started its takeoff run.

There appeared to be no reason a flying boat version of the Model 37 could not be developed. But the age of the flying boat was past, and Pan

Am decided to concentrate on more conventional aircraft such as the Constellation and DC-7.

FIRST FLIGHT

The single XC-99 was built at the Consolidated factory in San Diego, although the wings and other common B-36 parts were manufactured in Fort Worth and shipped to San Diego for installation. On 23 November 1947 the XC-99 made its maiden flight with Russell R. Rogers and Beryl A. Erickson at the controls.[10] The aircraft used the same 110-inch-diameter single main wheels as the XB-36, but these could

The lower aft cargo compartment had two observer stations so that crew members could monitor the engine and landing gear performance during takeoff and landing. The aft gunners performed a similar function in the B-36, in both cases mainly because the pilots had no direct visibility. (Convair via the San Diego Aerospace Museum)

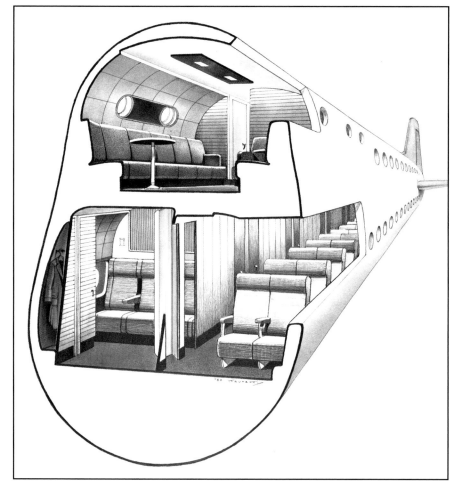

The double-deck Pan Am aircraft would have been very comfortable compared to other passenger aircraft of the era. Interestingly, the double-deck feature would influence some of Pan Am's future decisions, particularly concerning the early 747 development. (Convair via the San Diego Aerospace Museum)

be tolerated by the runway at Lindberg Field as long as the aircraft was lightly loaded. The four-wheel main gear was retrofitted, and the XC-99 first flew with it on 24 January 1949. Initially the aircraft was fitted with –25 engines, but in early 1950 was fitted with –41 engines for commonality with the B-36 fleet.

Like the B-36s, the XC-99 used unpowered flight controls. The control surfaces had an area almost equal to the entire wing area of a B-24, and were operated by a series of spring tabs that used air pressure to deflect the control surface. The spring tabs, looking much like normal trim tabs only larger, were directly operated by moving the control sticks in the cockpit, and caused the larger control surface to move via aerodynamic forces. The use of spring tabs was not original to the B-36/XC-99, but it was the largest aircraft ever equipped with the devices. Also like the early B-36s, the XC-99 used aluminum skin for the elevators, but doped fabric for the ailerons and rudder. Unlike the B-36, most of the XC-99 fuselage was of conventional alu-

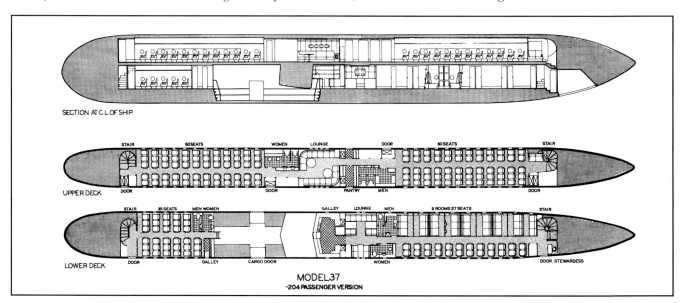

The interior layout of the landplane version of the Model 37 for Pan Am. (Convair via the San Diego Aerospace Museum)

minum construction, with magnesium used only for the tail cone and parts of the cargo doors. [11]

The XC-99 was equipped with two electrically-operated sliding cargo doors on the bottom of the fuselage, one just forward of the wing and one in the aft fuselage. The doors were supported by rollers that moved in tracks, and the fuselage skin had slots to accommodate the door brackets while they moved. The slots were covered flush by spring-loaded strips when the doors were closed. Two pairs of clamshell doors were installed immediately aft of the rear sliding cargo door although the rear sliding door had to be opened before them. Structural limitation prohibited the clamshell doors from being opened in flight, although either sliding door could be opened in order to drop cargo. Either cargo opening could be fitted with angled ramps that permitted vehicles to be driven onto the lower level.

There were two cargo compartments on the lower deck, separated by the wing carry-through structure, and a single long compartment on the upper deck.

Convair built a complete set of mockups for Pan Am's Model 37 "Super Clippers" in the closing days of World War II. The interior reflected the attitude of air travel that had existed prior to the war – that it should be luxurious and mimic the large ocean liners in the level of service. This is obviously reflected in the size and furnishings of the lavatories (top) and lounge. Note the lack of windows in the lounge – Convair was unsure how many windows could be installed in a pressurized fuselage without compromising its structural integrity. (Convair via the San Diego Aerospace Museum)

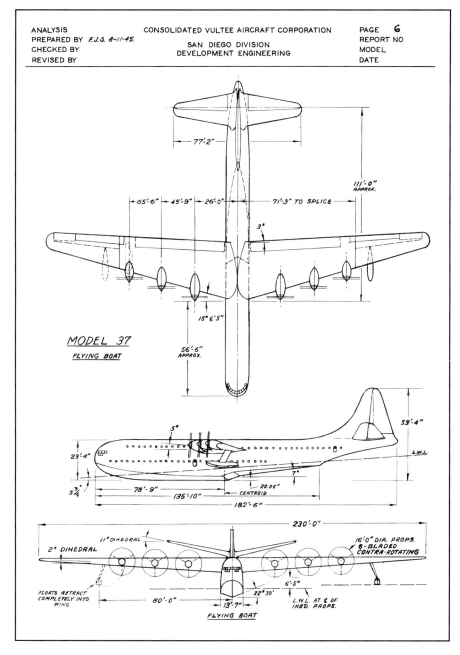

ANALYSIS
PREPARED BY *F.J.S. 8-11-45.*
CHECKED BY
REVISED BY

CONSOLIDATED VULTEE AIRCRAFT CORPORATION
SAN DIEGO DIVISION
DEVELOPMENT ENGINEERING

PAGE **6**
REPORT NO
MODEL
DATE

Pan American World Airways asked Convair to investigate a flying boat variant of the XC-99 for possible use after World War II. Pan Am had a great deal of experience flying long over-water routes using flying boats such as the Boeing 314 "Clippers," but was finally convinced that the future was in landplanes. The flying boat XC-99 was never built, and Pan Am went on to order the Lockheed Constellation and Douglas DC-7. (Convair via the San Diego Aerospace Museum)

Cargo could be loaded, unloaded, or shifted within the cargo compartments by means of four electric hoists. The hoist in each of the lower compartments could be used to shift or drop cargo while the aircraft was in flight, but the two hoists in the upper compartment were normally restricted to ground operations. The hoists were set on tracks located in the ceiling of each compartment and could traverse the entire length of their compartment. Each hoist could lift up to 4,000 pounds single purchase, or 8,000 pounds double purchase. The lower decks were equipped with winches attached to the cargo floor to pull items up the ramps.[12]

The upper cargo compartment was accessed via two openings in its floor, one directly above the forward sliding door, and the other directly above the aft-most clamshell door. There was also a ladder at the front and rear of the fuselage to allow personnel access to the upper compartment. Heat exchangers used waste engine heat to provide comfort air to the cargo compartments and flight deck. These heat exchangers could provide up to 4,800,000 BTUs per hour, enough to heat a 600-room hotel, yet the equipment weighed only 1,530 pounds.[13]

The flight deck was equipped with five canvas bunks, two of which could be reconfigured to provide "jump-type" seats along one of the outside walls. A toilet and drinking water supply were also provided, but no galley was fitted. Provisions were made for five additional toilets (two on the upper deck and three on the lower deck) when the aircraft was outfitted as a troop carrier. Troop seating was on canvas benches along each side of the fuselage on both decks.

The XC-99 was officially delivered to the Air Force on 26 May 1949 and was used extensively by the San Antonio Air Materiel Depot at Kelly AFB, Texas. In June 1950 the XC-99 made several 1,150-mile flights carrying B-36 parts from Kelly AFB to San Diego as part of Operation ELEPHANT. On 14 July, a return trip from San Diego to Kelly included ten R-4360 engines and 16 propellers, as well as other material. The total payload was 101,266 pounds, and the air-

craft had a ramp weight of 303,334 pounds. During the flight, the No. 6 engine began backfiring and was shut down – the flight was completed on five engines!

During January 1952 the aircraft flew 15 cargo flights totaling 117.25 hours carrying 1,123,000 pounds of cargo. It took an average of 54 minutes to load each 10,000 pounds of cargo with a ten-man loading crew. Offloading averaged just over half as long. The totals for a nine-month period around the same time were also impressive: 7,000,000 pounds of cargo during 115 flights, 65 of which were over 1,500 miles.[14]

The XC-99 continued to provide useful service to the San Antonio depot, and flew more flight hours than any other Air Force experimental aircraft. By June 1957 it was obvious that some structural fatigue was occurring, and the Air Force did not want to spend the estimated $1,000,000 to fix it. The XC-99 was permanently grounded. A few months later, title for the aircraft was transferred to the Disabled American Veterans, who put the aircraft on public display for the next 30 years. The aircraft fell into disrepair, and in 1993 the Kelly Field Heritage Foundation purchased it for $65,000 and donated it to the Air Force Museum. It currently sits on the ramp at the former Kelly AFB, its future uncertain.

By December 1949 Convair had designed a definitive production version of the C-99. The most visible change was the raised "bubble" cockpit common with the production B-36. This included the same basic flight deck used on the B-36B. A new nose landing gear was located in a bulge located under the forward fuselage, looking much like the radome under the B-36. The new

Built-in hoists allowed cargo to be loaded onto either deck of the XC-99 via large hatches in the bottom of the fuselage. Alternately, ramps could be installed that allowed some items to be driven up onto the lower decks. (Convair)

The XC-99 at an open house. Note the stair leading into the aft cargo doors and the uniquely painted propeller hubs. (San Diego Aerospace Museum Collection)

arrangement did not protrude into the cargo area, and its slightly longer stroke allowed a level floor (the XC-99 had a slight forward slope).[15]

A revised fuselage featured a rearranged cargo area with a pressurized upper deck that could accommodate 183 troops. The lower compartment remained unpressurized, but now featured large clamshell doors in the nose and tail that allowed vehicles to drive on and off at the same time. The doors provided an entrance measuring 12x13 feet and could accommodate the Army's 240-mm howitzer and M46 heavy tank. The C-99 was designed to allow vehicles or tanks to be transported with their operating and maintenance crews directly to a combat area without the need for a staging area, a capability not realized until the advent of the Lockheed C-5A Galaxy.

The C-99 had 21,714 cubic feet of available cargo space, compared to the 16,000 cubic feet available on the XC-99. The Fort Worth-based design team believed that 100,000 pounds could be transported 3,800 miles, with an overload capability of 116,000 pounds over a somewhat shorter distance. If necessary the aircraft could carry 401 fully-equipped troops (unpressurized) or 343 litters and 33 medical attendants. The aircraft shared the 230-foot wingspan of the standard B-36, but was 182 feet long and 57 feet high at the vertical stabilizer. The maximum gross takeoff weight was 357,000 pounds. Alternate designs were also prepared using the VDT engines proposed for the B-36C,

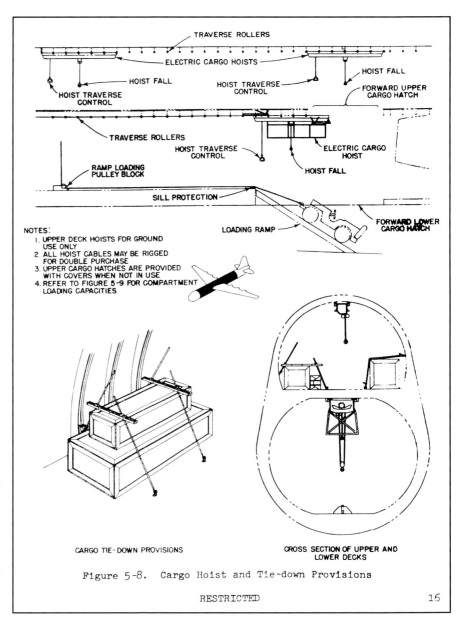

Figure 5-8. Cargo Hoist and Tie-down Provisions

RESTRICTED   16

The cargo loading and hoisting diagram from the flight handbook. (U.S. Air Force)

and also using the track-style landing gear tested on the XB-36.

But for reasons that are not readily apparent, the Air Force decided against procuring the C-99. Instead it bought large numbers of the Boeing C/KC-97 (a B-50 variant) and Douglas C-124 and C-133 transports.

None of these aircraft were as capable as the C-99 would have been, but at the time it was not completely obvious how much the U.S. military would come to rely on air transport. Of course, much of the reliance would wait until the advent of workable jet transports such as the Boeing C-135 and Lockheed C-141.

[1] Marcelle Size Knaack, *Post-World War II Bombers*, Office of Air Force History, 1988, p 8. [2] Aviation Week, 2 June 1952, p 12. [3] Convair XC-99 Press Book, undated, p 18. [4] Flight Operating Instructions for the XC-99 Airplane, 31 March 1949. [5] Convair Field Service Letter No. 56, 11 June 1951. [6] Convair XC-99 Press Book, undated, p 30. [7] *Ibid*, p 26. [8] Convair report ZD-37-004, *CVAC Model 37 for Pan American Airways*, 15 February 1945. [9] Convair report ZH-026, *A Comparison of Performance Between the Model 37 and a Flying Boat Version of the Same Airplane*, 17 August 1945. [10] Convair XC-99 Press Book, undated, p 1. [11] *Ibid*, p 11. [12] *Ibid*, p 20. [13] *Ibid*, p 28. [14] Aviation Week, 2 June 1952, p 12. [15] Aviation Week, 5 December 1949, p 14.

The lack of bumps on the inboard upper wing surfaces indicates this photo was taken while the XC-99 still had the original 110-inch main landing gear. Note the "Convair XC-99" emblem on the forward fuselage, and the lack of "SAAMA" markings on the tail. (Convair via the Terry Panopalis Collection)

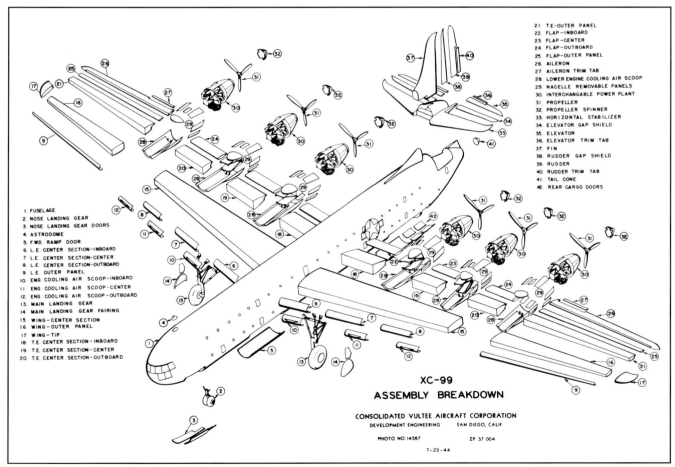

1. FUSELAGE
2. NOSE LANDING GEAR
3. NOSE LANDING GEAR DOORS
4. ASTRODOME
5. FWD. RAMP DOOR
6. L.E. CENTER SECTION—INBOARD
7. L.E. CENTER SECTION—CENTER
8. L.E. CENTER SECTION—OUTBOARD
9. L.E. OUTER PANEL
10. ENG. COOLING AIR SCOOP—INBOARD
11. ENG. COOLING AIR SCOOP—CENTER
12. ENG. COOLING AIR SCOOP—OUTBOARD
13. MAIN LANDING GEAR
14. MAIN LANDING GEAR FAIRING
15. WING—CENTER SECTION
16. WING—OUTER PANEL
17. WING—TIP
18. T.E. CENTER SECTION—INBOARD
19. T.E. CENTER SECTION—CENTER
20. T.E. CENTER SECTION—OUTBOARD

21. T.E.—OUTER PANEL
22. FLAP—INBOARD
23. FLAP—CENTER
24. FLAP—OUTBOARD
25. FLAP—OUTER PANEL
26. AILERON
27. AILERON TRIM TAB
28. LOWER ENGINE COOLING AIR SCOOP
29. NACELLE REMOVABLE PANELS
30. INTERCHANGABLE POWER PLANT
31. PROPELLER
32. PROPELLER SPINNER
33. HORIZONTAL STABILIZER
34. ELEVATOR GAP SHIELD
35. ELEVATOR
36. ELEVATOR TRIM TAB
37. FIN
38. RUDDER GAP SHIELD
39. RUDDER
40. RUDDER TRIM TAB
41. TAIL CONE
42. REAR CARGO DOORS

XC-99
ASSEMBLY BREAKDOWN

CONSOLIDATED VULTEE AIRCRAFT CORPORATION
DEVELOPMENT ENGINEERING   SAN DIEGO, CALIF.
PHOTO NO. 14587   ZP 37.004
7-23-44

Most of the XC-99 components other than the fuselage itself were common to the B-36, and were manufactured in Fort Worth and shipped to San Diego for final assembly. (Convair)

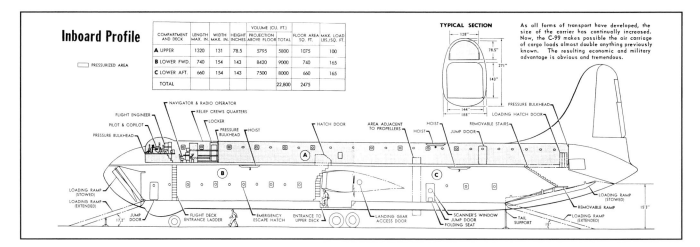

Inboard Profile

☐ PRESSURIZED AREA

COMPARTMENT AND DECK	LENGTH MAX. IN.	WIDTH MAX. IN.	HEIGHT INCHES	VOLUME (CU. FT.)		FLOOR AREA SQ. FT.	MAX. LOAD LBS./SQ. FT.
				PROJECTION ABOVE FLOOR	TOTAL		
A UPPER	1320	131	78.5	5795	5800	1075	100
B LOWER FWD.	740	154	143	8420	9000	740	165
C LOWER AFT.	660	154	143	7500	8000	660	165
TOTAL					22,800	2475	

TYPICAL SECTION

As all forms of transport have developed, the size of the carrier has continually increased. Now, the C-99 makes possible the air carriage of cargo loads almost double anything previously known. The resulting economic and military advantage is obvious and tremendous.

Interior arrangement of the proposed production C-99 military transport. (Lockheed Martin)

The weather radar changed the whole character of the XC-99's nose, although the actual change was relatively minor. Note the large opening side windows on the flight deck. (U.S. Air Force via the San Diego Aerospace Museum)

Late in its operational service, the XC-99 was fitted with weather radar on the nose, and the top of the crew compartment was painted white as a measure of protection against the Texas sun. Photographed on 15 May 1953. (A. Kreiger via the Norm Taylor Collection via Richard Freeman)

INITIAL PRODUCTION

B-36A, B-36B, AND THE ABORTIVE B-36C

The B-36A was essentially similar to the preceding YB-36, including the use of 3,000-hp R-4360-25 Wasp Major engines. The first aircraft (44-92004) made its maiden flight on 28 August 1947, actually beating the YB-36 into the air by almost four months. This aircraft was later redesignated YB-36A, and was only fitted with enough equipment for a single flight to Wright Field where it was used as a structural loads airframe and tested to destruction. The aircraft was flown to Wright Field simply because nobody could figure out another method of getting it there. A total of 7 hours and 36 minutes of flight time were accumulated during its two flights (it had flown once at Fort Worth just to prove it was airworthy).

The planned APG-7 bombing/navigation system had been superceded by a better packaged APQ-23 with a radome located beneath the forward fuselage where the lower gun turrets were originally going to be located. The complex General Electric defensive armament system was not fully developed and was not initially installed on any of the B-36As. However, parts of the system were installed in the original YB-36 and various A-models for testing, although none of the aircraft ever had a complete system.

The normal crew complement was listed as 15, but this included eight gunners who had no guns. The other seven crew members were a pilot, copilot, radar-bombardier, navigator, flight engineer, and two radiomen.

On 13–14 May 1948, a single B-36A (44-92013) conducted a simulated long-range tactical mission. The aircraft had a gross weight of 299,619 pounds, including 10,000 pounds of simulated bombs, 5,796 pounds of

The Air Force and Convair took great delight in showing how large the B-36 was. Here a B-36A poses with a B-17, B-29, and B-18 on the ramp at Fort Worth. (Lockheed Martin)

The first delivery to SAC was on 26 June 1948, and the last B-36A was accepted in February 1949.[2]

The height of the B-36 vertical stabilizer was greater than the height of the plant door. The solution – raise the nose of the aircraft in order to lower the tail, then tow it outside. Note the extended tail bumper under the rear fuselage of this red-tailed B-36B. The tail bumper was a feature of the A- and B-models, but would not be included in later aircraft. (Convair)

As built (without defensive armament) the B-36As had a ramp weight of 310,380 pounds when loaded with 24,121 gallons of fuel and 10,000 pounds of bombs. They required a takeoff run of 8,000 feet, and had a realistic radius of action of 3,880 miles (i.e., they could hit a target 3,880 miles away, and return). Over the target they had a maximum speed of 345 mph at 31,600 feet, and a service ceiling of 39,100 feet – not quite up to the original specification, but still impressive for 1948.

Even more impressive was the bomb load. On 30 June 1948, a B-36A dropped 72,000 pounds of bombs during a test flight, the heaviest bomb load yet carried by any bomber.[3] The four bomb bays were covered by magnesium doors that slid up the outside of the fuselage when opened, much like those used on the B-24. The doors were slow to operate, tended to stick in the extremely cold temperatures at 40,000 feet, and significantly increased drag when open. A better solution would need to be found.

Another view of a B-36 being towed from the assembly line. The extreme angle necessary for the vertical stabilizer to clear the building door is evident here. Note the lack of a buzz number on the forward fuselage, and the small UNITED STATES AIR FORCE markings in its place. The "40" on the nose is the manufacturing sequence number, but was normally scratched-out by the censor as restricted information. (Convair via the San Diego Aerospace Museum)

simulated 20-mm ammunition, and ballast to compensate for the lack of turrets and other items of equipment not fitted to the B-36As. The flight duration was 36 hours and 8 minutes during which 8,062 miles were flown at an average 223 mph. The aircraft landed with 986 gallons of fuel remaining, which could have extended the mission by 508 miles.[1]

On 18 June 1948 A B-36A was delivered to Eglin AFB for climatic testing, which lasted most of the following year. A total of 19 B-36As were delivered to the 7th Bombard-

The B-36A suffered from many of the types of problems normally encountered when a complex new aircraft enters service. The fuel tanks leaked, the electrical system was troublesome, and engine cooling was still not as good as it should have been. None of the problems were insurmountable, and Convair engineers continued to work on solutions. Nevertheless, the service life of the B-36A was extremely

The assembly line in Building 4 while producing B-36As. The leading edge of the wing was removable (it hinged upwards also) for access to the fuel tanks (through the small square door on the nearest airplane). At the upper right is a monorail that ran the length of the factory to carry parts. After the wings were mated to the fuselage the B-36 had to angled since its 230-foot wingspan exceeded the 200-foot width of the building. (Lockheed Martin)

short, and all of them had been remanufactured into RB-36Es by July 1951.

B-36B

The B-36B used uprated 3,500-hp R-4360-41 engines with water injection, allowing slightly shorter take-off distances, and yielding marginally higher cruising speeds and a higher top speed. The first B-36B made its maiden flight on 8 July 1948 with Beryl Erickson at the con-

Two early B-36 forward fuselages in January 1947. The location of the nose turret, cockpit, and upper forward turret bay are clearly visible. (Convair)

The bottom turrets in the deployed position of a new B-36B undergoing testing at Eglin AFB, Florida. Note the large air conditioning hose at the extreme left – ground carts ducted cool air into the interior to help combat the Florida heat. (Lockheed Martin)

trols, and subsequent testing showed that its performance was generally better than expected. An average cruising speed of 300 mph could be maintained at 40,000 feet, and the aircraft could carry up to 86,000 pounds of bombs, a rather significant 14,000 pound increase over the B-36A. It appears that at least the first few B-36Bs were also equipped with the mounting brackets to carry the F-85 parasite fighter, although it is unlikely any equipment was actually installed.[4]

The B-36B used an AN/APQ-24 bombing/navigation system with an improved search radar and faster computer. In addition, the defensive armament was installed, making it the first true combat version of the B-36. The sixteen 20-mm cannon were installed in six retractable remotely-operated turrets each equipped with a pair of cannon, plus two more pairs in nose and tail turrets. This was the most formidable defensive armament yet fitted to any warplane. The guns were aimed

using computing gunsights situated at two blisters on the forward fuselage and four blisters on the aft fuselage. The tail turret was directed by an AN/APG-3 gun-laying radar.

Like the B-36A, the crew of the B-36B was normally fifteen, a pilot, copilot, radar-bombardier, navigator, flight engineer, two radiomen, three forward gunners, and five rear gunners. In this case the gunners actually had something to do.

Beginning in late November 1948 B-36Bs were assigned to the 7th BG(H) at Carswell AFB, which already operated the B-36As in a training role.[5] The 11th BG(H) would also be activated at Carswell with the B-36B. However, the Cold War dictated that bases closer to the Soviet Union be found in order to shorten the response time and allow deeper penetration. After Project GEM (global electronics modification) provided suitable polar navigation equipment, the 7th BG(H) began deploying B-36Bs to bases near Goose Bay, Labrador; Limestone, Maine; and Fairbanks, Alaska. These aircraft had their tails and wingtips painted bright red in case they were forced down in the rough terrain (day-glo paint had not been perfected yet).

In a maximum range demonstration, a B-36B from the 7th BG(H) flew a 35-hour round-trip simulated bombing mission from Carswell to Hawaii on 7-8 December 1948. A 10,000 pound load of dummy bombs was dropped in the ocean a short distance from Hawaii. The flight covered over 8,100 miles, although the average cruising speed was only 236 mph. Nevertheless, this proved the B-36 was a true intercontinental bomber and, given the right circumstance, could attack almost any tar-

More air conditioning – this time into the forward compartment. Note the open doors on the upper turret bay. (Lockheed Martin)

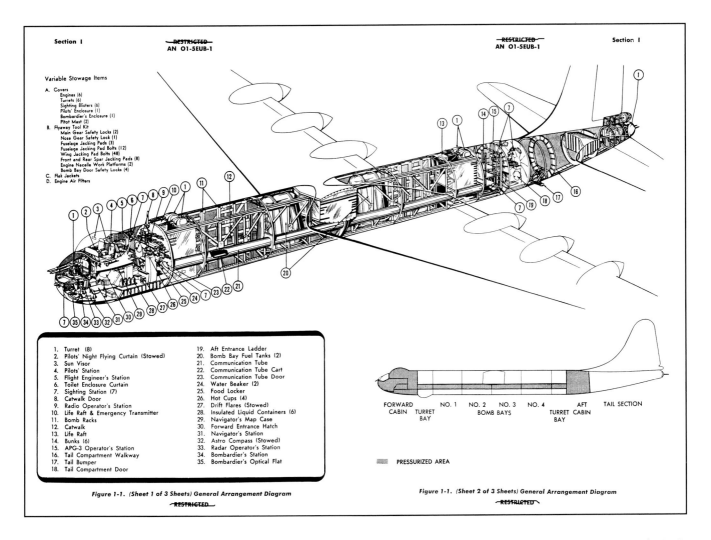

Section I

RESTRICTED
AN 01-5EUB-1

RESTRICTED
AN 01-5EUB-1

Section I

Variable Stowage Items

A. Covers
 Engines (6)
 Turrets (6)
 Sighting Blisters (6)
 Pilots' Enclosure (1)
 Bombardier's Enclosure (1)
 Pitot Mast (2)
B. Flyaway Tool Kit
 Main Gear Safety Locks (2)
 Nose Gear Safety Lock (1)
 Fuselage Jacking Pads (3)
 Fuselage Jacking Pad Bolts (12)
 Wing Jacking Pad Bolts (48)
 Front and Rear Spar Jacking Pads (8)
 Engine Nacelle Work Platforms (2)
 Bomb Bay Door Safety Locks (4)
C. Flak Jackets
D. Engine Air Filters

1. Turret (8)	19. Aft Entrance Ladder
2. Pilots' Night Flying Curtain (Stowed)	20. Bomb Bay Fuel Tanks (2)
3. Sun Visor	21. Communication Tube
4. Pilots' Station	22. Communication Tube Cart
5. Flight Engineer's Station	23. Communication Tube Door
6. Toilet Enclosure Curtain	24. Water Beaker (2)
7. Sighting Station (7)	25. Food Locker
8. Catwalk Door	26. Hot Cups (4)
9. Radio Operator's Station	27. Drift Flares (Stowed)
10. Life Raft & Emergency Transmitter	28. Insulated Liquid Containers (6)
11. Bomb Racks	29. Navigator's Map Case
12. Catwalk	30. Forward Entrance Hatch
13. Life Raft	31. Navigator's Station
14. Bunks (6)	32. Astro Compass (Stowed)
15. APG-3 Operator's Station	33. Radar Operator's Station
16. Tail Compartment Walkway	34. Bombardier's Station
17. Tail Bumper	35. Bombardier's Optical Flat
18. Tail Compartment Door	

FORWARD CABIN   TURRET BAY   NO. 1   NO. 2   NO. 3   NO. 4   AFT TURRET CABIN BAY   BOMB BAYS   TAIL SECTION

▨ PRESSURIZED AREA

Figure 1-1. (Sheet 1 of 3 Sheets) General Arrangement Diagram
RESTRICTED

Figure 1-1. (Sheet 2 of 3 Sheets) General Arrangement Diagram
RESTRICTED

The general arrangement diagram from the B-36B flight manual. Note the auxiliary fuel tanks in bomb bay No. 2 and No. 3. (U.S. Air Force)

get in the world. Interestingly, the B-36 penetrated Hawaiian airspace without being detected by the defensive forces on the islands, an embarrassment they did not appreciate, coming seven years to the day after the attack on Pearl Harbor.

More demonstrations followed. On 29 June 1948, a B-36B established a record bomb lift by taking a pair of dummy 43,000-pound Grand Slam bombs aloft at Muroc AFB (now Edwards AFB). The first was released at an altitude of 35,000 feet, the second from 41,000 feet, and the entire flight covered 3,100 miles. In March 1949, a B-36B established a distance record of 9,600 miles flown

Part of the servicing problem was corrected with maintenance docks. This is a rear view of half of an all-weather service dock built by Convair. The complete dock consisted of four sections, each 36 feet in depth and 60 feet in length. Two different types of docks were built. The first style was set up permanently on the ramp in front of the Fort Worth and San Diego plants, and the San Antonio depot. The other style was mobile and could be moved as necessary. (Convair via the San Diego Aerospace Museum)

The bulges on the landing gear doors to cover the four-wheel bogies were very prominent. The radome under the forward fuselage housed the AN/APS-23 search radar used by the bomb/nav system. Many of the early B-36s had their tails painted red while they operated in the Arctic region. Usually the wing tips were also painted red, but at least the bottom of these are not. Note the location of the national insignia and buzz number on the underside of the wings. (Convair via the San Diego Aerospace Museum)

in 43 hours 37 minutes, with enough fuel remaining for two more hours of flying. The B-36 had been carrying a simulated load of 10,000 pounds, and encountered severe headwinds over the Rocky Mountains. A 10,000-mile mission was undoubtedly possible under ideal conditions.[6] And remember, this was before in-flight refueling – the B-36 could remain aloft for nearly two days, totally self sufficient.

Still, everything was not working as well as it could be. The APQ-24 was neither as reliable nor as accurate in service as it had been during testing. The problem was eventually traced to faulty vacuum tubes and inadequate crew training. The complex General Electric remotely-controlled turrets were prone to frequent failures. Although conceptually similar to the defensive armament installed on the B-29, the system was much more complex, a necessity to ensure it was capable of handling the ever increasing speeds of the fighters it was designed to shoot down. The extreme cold at 40,000 feet created

An unarmed B-36A (44-92009) on 15 April 1948. Note the "bullet" antenna under the nose – this was later replaced by a small streamlined fairing that was almost flush with the fuselage. The large buzz number on the forward fuselage was used by most early B-36s. Like most early B-36s, the tail turret is a dummy unit. (Lockheed Martin)

problems. The APG-3 gun-laying radar for the tail turret also proved to be remarkably troublesome. As late as February of 1950, the commander of the 8th Air Force was complaining that "… there was little point in driving a B-36 around carrying a lot of guns that didn't work."

Many of the B-36B's initial problems resembled those of any other new and complex aircraft. Parts shortages were acute, and it was often necessary to cannibalize some B-36Bs to keep others flying. The problems seemed larger than normal, but the B-36 was a larger than normal aircraft. Equipment such as empennage stands, dollies, and jacks were in short supply. Because there was no funding for new equipment, maintenance crews utilized some of the tools and equipment left over from the old B-29s. Personnel turnover in the postwar environment further hampered progress. The aircraft were constantly being reconfigured or awaiting modification, and in reality, an operational capability was not achieved until 1952.

In his book, Meyers Jacobsen mentions one of the more interesting problems encountered by the B-36 units at Carswell. When a part was needed that was manufactured by Convair, which was located a mile across the runway, the 7th BG(H) had to request the part from the Air Materiel Command depot at San Antonio, which in turn requested it

Even the 56-inch tires on the revised main landing gear were large. Note the deployed flap – the B-36 flaps were multi-segmented due to the placement of the pusher engines. (San Diego Aerospace Museum Collection)

An observer's dome, in the roof of the bubble cockpit, allowed the navigator to perform celestial navigation. Note the two wire antennas, one on either side of the fuselage, stretching to the tail. (Peter M. Bowers)

from Convair. Convair then shipped the part to San Antonio, which turned around and shipped it to Carswell. Finally, somebody in the Air Force realized the irony of the situation, and allowed Convair to drive the parts across the ramp and deliver them to the B-36 units.

An assembly line shot of a B-36B shows the location for the nose turret, the crew access hatch, the forward sighting blister, and the upper forward turret bay. The outer wing panels have not yet been installed. (Lockheed Martin)

When the B-36B started entering the SAC inventory in the fall of 1948, the Air Force had 59 groups, with an eventual goal of 70 groups. An unexpected decision by President Truman to hold the 1949 defense budget to a ceiling of $11 billion was a serious blow. The problem was no longer how to procure additional aircraft for 70 groups, but how to whittle current forces to 48 groups with the least possible harm to national security. Cancelling the aircraft already on order, with minimum charges to the government, was a difficult task. In the end, over $573 million in contracts were cancelled, costing the government $56 million in penalties.[7]

Surprisingly, the B-36 actually gained from the crisis. The Air Force cancelled the purchase of various bombers, fighters, and transports, but at the same time, endorsed the urgent procurement of additional B-36s. A few months later, the Boeing B-54 (an improved B-50) was cancelled in favor of more RB-36s.

The three military services began to squabble over which programs were most important. The Air Force and the Navy had long recognized that whichever service possessed the atomic mission would eventually receive a larger share of the budget. Thus, they had grown more of each other's strategic programs.

The B-36 program was the subject of a lot of criticism, especially from the Navy. It was accused of being as slow as the B-24 and far more vulnerable to attack by modern fighters. Since the B-36 had been one of the few survivors in the mass cancellations of early 1949, anonymous reports had begun to circulate charging that undue favoritism and corruption were involved in awarding the B-36 contracts.

At the time, the Secretary of Defense was Louis A. Johnson, a former director at Convair. On 23 April 1949, just a month after entering office, Johnson abruptly cancelled the Navy's first supercarrier, the USS *United States* (CVA-58), which had been ordered by his predecessor to allow the Navy to develop a strategic bombing capability. Funds from the cancellation were used largely to order more B-36s. The Navy was enraged at the cancellation, but the Air Force insisted that strategic bombing was strictly an Air Force responsibility. The decision was justified on the basis that the government could not afford both new strategic bombers and a new carrier force. The B-36 had already demonstrated it was capable of reaching targets inside the Soviet Union, while the entire concept of carrier-borne nuclear bombers had yet to be proven.

On 1 May 1949, however, the Soviets publicly demonstrated the MiG-15 jet-powered fighter, and there were serious doubts that the B-36 could defend itself against the new fighter. Many officers expressed concerns that the Air Force had spent a fortune on what would turn out to be a sitting duck. An anonymous document began making the rounds in press and congressional circles charging that the aircraft's performance did not live up to Air Force claims.

In June 1949, the House Armed Services Committee opened an investigation of what came to be known in the press as the "B-36 Affair." On 25 August the House committee cleared the Air Force and Convair of any misconduct. Although the B-36 contract survived unscathed, one of the results of these hearings was an amendment to the National Security Act of 1947 which enlarged and

The 53rd B-36 shows a typical early nose. Note the lack of cannon in the nose turret and the glazed bombardier window. Once aircraft began receiving the Y-3 periscopic bomb sight, the glazed window was normally covered over and the windshield wiper removed. (Lockheed Martin)

strengthened the office of the Secretary of Defense and severely weakened the authority of the individual service secretaries.[8]

It was not over. In October 1949 congressional hearings resumed, this time on the question of whether the defense of the United States should

An aft fuselage being assembled prior to being mated with the rest of the airframe. One of the hatches in the forward bulkhead was used by the communications tube; the other provided access to the aft turret bay. (Lockheed Martin)

A red-tailed B-36B (44-92039) was on display in Chicago during 1949. Noteworthy is the aerodynamic shape of the early ECM antennas under the forward sighting blister. (Peter M. Bowers)

rely on the Air Force's strategic bombers or the Navy's proposed fleet of aircraft carriers. It resulted in nearly open warfare between the Air Force and the Navy over who would control the nuclear mission. The Air Force argued that it had already demonstrated its ability to perform the mission, while the Navy continued to argue over the technical obsolescence of the B-36. The Navy was still enraged at the cancellation of the *United States*, and Admiral Arthur W.

Radford, Commander-in-Chief (CinC) of the Pacific Fleet, denounced the B-36 as a "billion dollar blunder," a quote that was picked up by many newspapers across the country. Although there were still doubts about the B-36's ability to survive enemy fighter attack, the program once again survived uncut.

Thankfully, the B-36B was proving to be a capable, if somewhat slow aircraft. The Air Force and Convair

were both looking for ways to improve the speed of the B-36, and everybody concerned was working on improving the reliability of the aircraft and its systems. It was now obvious that B-36 production would exceed the original 100 aircraft order, and that the B-36 would be the Air Force's primary nuclear delivery aircraft until development of the jet-powered B-52, and all of its supporting infrastructure (tankers, etc.), was completed, something not expected until 1955 at the earliest.

Convair actually built 73 B-36Bs, but the Air Force directed 11 of them to be modified with jet engines prior to delivery – four of the 11 appeared on Air Force rolls as B-36Ds, and seven as RB-36Ds. Therefore, the Air Force formally accepted 62 B-36Bs –31 in FY49, 30 in FY50, and the last one in September 1950 (FY51).

By the time the last B-36B was accepted, some had already been returned to Convair to be converted to the B-36D configuration with the addition of four General Electric J47-GE-19 turbojets paired in pods underneath the outer wings. The B-36B phaseout from service was almost as quick as that of the B-36A. Twenty-five B-36Bs were already undergoing conversion during the first half of 1951, and the last of the 60 converted B-36Bs were redelivered during February 1952. Two of the bombers had crashed before they could be converted.

B-36C

Even though the B-36's performance since mid-1948 was exceeding early expectations, the aircraft's relatively slow speed continued to cause concern. Tests had shown that altitude was very important in protecting a

The classic shot of B-36s over the Capitol Building in Washington, D.C. symbolized the raging debate between the Air Force and Navy over who would control the strategic mission in the early 1950s. (Lockheed Martin)

WARBIRD**TECH**
S E R I E S

The YB-36A (44-92004) only made two flights – one airworthiness flight at Fort Worth, and its delivery flight from Fort Worth to Wright Field in Ohio. Once at Wright Field the airframe was used for structural tests, and was eventually tested to destruction. The aircraft carried only minimal equipment on its two flights – note the lack of a search radar radome under the forward fuselage. The original YB-36 took the place of the aircraft when the RB-36E conversions were approved. (Convair via the San Diego Aerospace Museum)

bomber, and the B-36 excelled at flying high. Nevertheless, a burst of speed over a target or while under attack increased a bomber's chances of survival.

In March 1947, Convair proposed that 34 aircraft out of the original 100 be completed as B-36Cs powered by 4,300-hp R-4360-51 Variable Discharge Turbine (VDT) Wasp Majors. In other applications, the VDT concept was known as a compound or turbocompound engine, and a variation of the concept was used very successfully on the Wright R-3350s used on the Douglas DC-7 transport.

At Wright Field, the YB-36A was slowly tested to destruction to determine its ultimate structural strength. At one point, the airframe had to be turned upside down so that loads could be applied to the bottom of the wings – the photo above shows it while being flipped. (via Ed Calvert via Don Pyeatt)

The B-36C would have presented a major change in the appearance of the B-36. Although the six engines remained in their normal locations behind the aft wing spar, extension shafts would have driven tractor propellers, a change necessitated by the configuration of the VDT engines. Very few images of the project remain. (Convair)

Unfortunately, the use of the engines would require a change from a pusher to a tractor configuration, entailing a significant redesign of some structure, including what amounted to a new wing. Although the engine would remain in its normal position behind the main wing spar, its orientation would be changed to face forward, and it would drive tractor propellers through 10-foot shafts that extended through the wing. In the VDT, exhaust gases from the engine would pass through a General Electric CHM-2 turbosupercharger with a clamshell nozzle that created jet thrust by varying the size of the turbine exit.

Convair claimed that the VDT engine (also proposed for the B-50) would give the B-36 a top speed of 410 mph and a 45,000-foot service ceiling. To offset the cost of adapting the VDT engine to the B-36, Convair suggested deleting three B-36s from the current procurement contract. This was approved in July 1947. Convair hoped additional VDT-equipped B-36Cs would be ordered if the prototype proved successful, but a decision on this matter was deferred.

A new Aircraft and Weapons Board met for the first time on 19 August, and strategic bombing was the first subject to be reviewed. Some board members considered the B-36 obsolete and wanted to concentrate on fast jet bombers, an obvious gamble since early models would have very limited range and would not be available for several years. Others supported installing the new VDT engines on the B-36 and using it as a general-purpose bomber. Still others preferred the B-50 because it was faster than the B-36. After prolonged discussion, a consensus emerged to retain the B-36 as a nuclear bomber that would eventually be replaced by the B-52, and to produce the B-50 as an interim general-purpose bomber to be replaced by the B-47. Given this, there was no particular reason to install the VDT engine in a prototype B-36, and no additional B-36 procurement would be needed. The board's recommendation was approved, and the B-36C prototype was cancelled on 22 August 1947.

The cancellation of the prototype did not stop Convair from proposing that the last 34 B-36s in the original contract be completed as B-36Cs. Convair estimated that the extra cost of the B-36Cs could be met by reducing the overall procurement to only 95 B-36s, and that the B-36Cs could be produced without delaying the program by more than six months. It was even suggested that the remaining B-36A and B aircraft could be retrofitted to B-36C standards, although no details were forthcoming on how to accomplish this. The Convair proposal for the 34 new-build B-36Cs was accepted on 5 December 1947, however, no decision was made on retrofitting the 61 existing B-36s.

Unfortunately, the B-36C project quickly ran into technical difficulties. There were problems with engine cooling generated by the aircraft's high-operating altitude, which subsequently degraded the engine's power and made Convair's earlier performance estimates unachievable. By the spring of 1948,

it had become apparent that the B-36C was not going to materialize, and the Air Force once again considered canceling the entire B-36 program. By this time, some in SAC had lost faith in the B-36 as a long-range strategic bomber, and believed this relatively slow aircraft would be useful only for such tasks as sea-search or reconnaissance.

Much of this was based on emotion and misinformation. A series of evaluations in mid-1948 showed that the standard B-36B surpassed the B-50 in cruising speed at very long range (mainly because the B-50 had to slow down to refuel), had a higher service and cruise ceiling, a larger payload capacity, and a much greater combat radius than the B-50 (assuming no refueling). It now seemed that the B-36 might be a better aircraft than anyone had expected, and that any hasty reduction in the program might be a mistake.

But it was probably the Soviets who were actually responsible for saving the B-36 program. On 18 June 1948, the Soviets began their blockade of Berlin. On 25 June 1948, Air Force Secretary W. Stuart Symington decided to continue the B-36 program since it was the only truly intercontinental bomber then available. General Kenney endorsed this decision, even though only a month earlier he had been recommending that the B-36 program be halted. The VDT-equipped B-36Cs that had been ordered would revert to standard B-36B configuration. Five aircraft still had to be cut from the original 100 aircraft order to meet inflation and to pay for the development costs of the ill-fated B-36C project.

This B-36A was assigned to the 7th BG(H) at Carswell AFB, across the field from the Convair plant. This was the first aircraft delivered to SAC. The name on the nose is "City of Fort Worth." (John Wegg via the San Diego Aerospace Museum)

B-36s undergoing modification at San Diego's Lindberg Field, which is located adjacent to San Diego Bay. Note the maintenance stands covering the wings on two of the B-36s on the right. (Convair via the San Diego Aerospace Museum)

[1] Convair report FZA-36-091, *Summary Report of B-36A Airplane Long Range Simulated tactical Mission Flight Two*, 4 June 1948. [2] Marcelle Size Knack, *Post-World War II Bombers*, Office of Air Force History, 1988, p 21. [3] *Ibid*, p 23. [4] Aviation Week, 18 October 1948, p 12. [5] Marcelle Size Knack, *Post-World War II Bombers*, Office of Air Force History, 1988, p 25. [6] Aviation Week, 15 August 1949, p 14. [7] Aviation Week, 12 September 1949, p 37. [8] Marcelle Size Knack, *Post-World War II Bombers*, Office of Air Force History, 1988, p 27. [9] Aviation Week, 15 August 1949, p 14.

The official B-36B flight and maintenance manuals were not necessarily "politically correct" as these cartoons show. No doubt the cartoons served their purpose of enticing the crew to read them. (U.S. Air Force)

Because of its size and lifting capability, the B-36 was considered for many roles during its career. One of the less known is this proposal to use the bomber to carry an early concept of the Navaho missile. Note the early (J35) jet pods on the model, and that the aircraft in the drawing is a B-36B without jet pods. (Boeing Historical Archives Collection)

Special carriers were developed that would have allowed B-36s to transport two complete spare engines. In reality, these were two nacelles that were bolted back-to-back with a fairing between them. The pods were bolted onto the racks in bomb bay No. 1 – note the open sliding-type bomb bay doors. Unfortunately the carriers would not work with the newer-style snap-action bomb bay doors, and they were never adopted for operational use. (Convair via the San Diego Aerospace Museum)

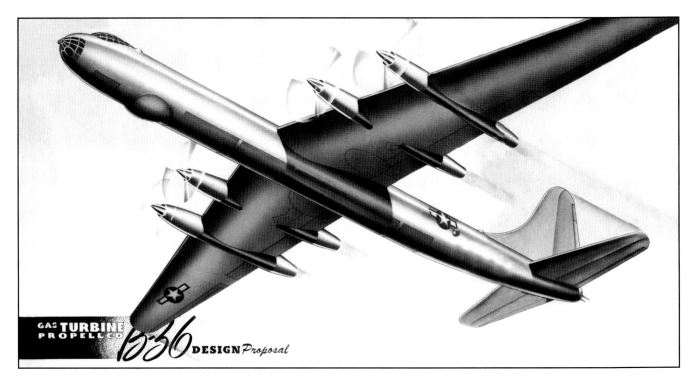

GAS **TURBINE** PROPELLED *B-36* DESIGN *Proposal*

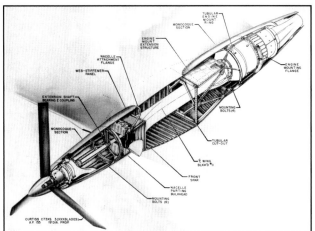

On 14 February 1947 Convair proposed to modify one B-36A (44-92049) with Curtiss-Wright XT35-W-1 gas turbine engines driving two tractor propellers on each wing. The engines were installed in the same locations normally used by the inboard and center Wasps, and the outer two engine nacelles would be deleted. Each engine was mounted aft of the rear spar with an extension shaft extending forward through the rear and front spars to a reduction gear box and a 19-foot diameter propeller. The installation was expected to cost less than $1.5 million, but was turned down by the Air Force because they believed, correctly, that the Curtiss-Wright schedule was overly optimistic. (Convair via the San Diego Aerospace Museum)

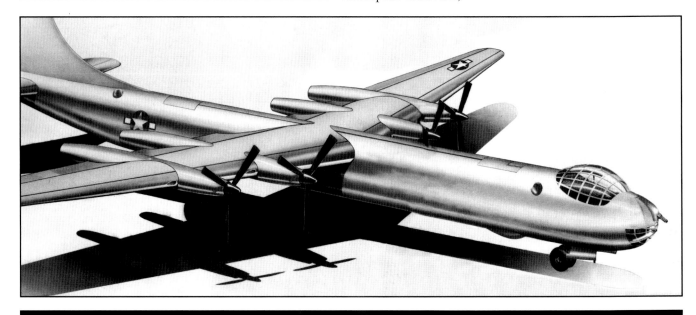

LATE PRODUCTION

During the 1950s, the government-owned plant at Fort Worth run by Convair (which now produces Lockheed F-16 fighters) occupied over 546 acres across the field from Carswell AFB. The buildings occupied 62 acres, with over 4,000,000 square feet of enclosed space and 8,500,000 square feet of paved working areas. An on-site environmental chamber could simulate altitudes as high as 60,000 feet and temperatures of –100 degF. The plant employed over 31,000 people while producing one B-36 per week (the average production for most of the run). The plant produced over 68,000 separate parts, in addition to those made by subcontractors. There were 57 major subcontractors (excluding Convair's San Diego plant) and 1,553 suppliers located in 36 states and the District of Columbia. A total of 2,500 machine tools and 126,500 production tools were used, and the assembly line integrated 8,500 separate subassemblies and 27 miles of wiring. The single B-36 line took up more space in the Fort Worth plant than had been occupied by two B-32 production lines during World War II.[1]

The original order for 100 (later reduced to 95) B-36s was based on a unit cost of $4,692,392 per aircraft, of which nearly 50 percent was government-furnished equipment. The remanufacture and modification of these aircraft to RB-36E and B-36D standard added $1,556,294 per aircraft, for a total of $6,248,686. The second increment of 75 B-36s cost $4,732,939 per aircraft, including the new bomb/nav system and engines.

Part of this reduction was based on the write-off of the production tooling cost after the initial production run. The breakdown of these later aircraft was about 58.2 percent GFE and 41.8 percent Convair.[2]

B-36D

On 5 October 1948 Convair proposed installing two pairs of turbojet engines in pods underneath the outer wing panels of the B-36. These engines could be used during take-off and for short bursts of speed at critical times, and would have only a minimal effect on range.

Unlike the extensive changes needed to install the VDT engines on the still-borne B-36C, only minor modifications would be required to mount the jet nacelles. In fact, Convair was confident that a prototype B-36 with jet engines would be ready to fly less than four months after Air Force approval. The Air Force did not question the obvious merits of the Convair proposal, but approval was delayed by budgetary restrictions looming in December 1948, and the decision a month before to remanufacture the B-36As into RB-36E reconnaissance aircraft.

The engines selected were 5,200-lbf General Electric J47-GE-19 turbojets, although at least some early aircraft used –11 versions instead. The pods were essentially the same as those

MODEL	DESIGN G.W. (LBS)	PRESSURIZED CREW COMPARTMENTS	CREW	ENGINEER'S STATION	RECIP. ENGINES	WING FUEL TANKS	GUN TURRETS	BOMB BAYS	BOMBING SYSTEM
B-36D	357,500	2	15	SINGLE	R4360-41	8	8	4	K( ) & UNIVERSAL
B-36D-II	357,500	2	15	SINGLE	R4360-41	8	8	4	K( ) & UNIVERSAL
B-36D-III	357,500	2	13	SINGLE	R4360-41	8	1	4	K( ) & UNIVERSAL
B-36F	357,500	2	15	SINGLE	R4360-53	8	8	4	K( ) & UNIVERSAL
B-36F-II	357,500	2	15	SINGLE	R4360-53	8	8	4	K( ) & UNIVERSAL
B-36F-III	357,500	2	13	SINGLE	R4360-53	8	1	4	K( ) & UNIVERSAL
B-36H	357,500	2	15	DUAL	R4360-53	8	8	4	K( ) & UNIVERSAL
B-36H-II	357,500	2	15	DUAL	R4360-53	8	8	4	K( ) & UNIVERSAL
B-36H-III	357,500	2	13	DUAL	R4360-53	8	1	4	K( ) & UNIVERSAL
B-36J	410,000	2	13	DUAL	R4360-53	10	1	4	K( ) & UNIVERSAL
RB-36D & E	357,500	3	22	SINGLE	R4360-41	8	8	2	CONV. & UNIVERSAL
RB-36D & E-II	357,500	3	22	SINGLE	R4360-41	8	8	2	CONV. & UNIVERSAL
RB-36D & E-III	357,500	3	19	SINGLE	R4360-41	8	1	2	CONV. & UNIVERSAL
RB-36F	357,500	3	22	SINGLE	R4360-53	8	8	2	CONV. & UNIVERSAL
RB-36F-II	357,500	3	22	SINGLE	R4360-53	8	8	2	CONV. & UNIVERSAL
RB-36F-III	357,500	3	19	SINGLE	R4360-53	8	1	2	CONV. & UNIVERSAL
RB-36H	357,500	3	22	DUAL	R4360-53	8	8	2	CONV. & UNIVERSAL
RB-36H-II	357,500	3	22	DUAL	R4360-53	8	8	2	CONV. & UNIVERSAL
RB-36H-III	357,500	3	19	DUAL	R4360-53	8	1	2	CONV. & UNIVERSAL

Main Differences TABLE

75-102-A

The table from an RB-36H flight manual showing the primary differences between the operational B-36 models. (U.S. Air Force)

developed for the inboard engines on the Boeing B-47 Stratojet, except that the outrigger landing gear was deleted. Early pods were manufactured alongside B-47 pods, although eventually Bell (who made them under contract) eventually set up a new production line in Texas just for the B-36 program. Special collapsible aerodynamic covers were installed over the engine inlets to minimize drag when the engines were not operating. The engines were modified to burn standard aviation fuel instead of jet fuel so that the B-36 could feed them from the existing fuel supply. This resulted in the engines producing slightly less power than normal, but the trade-off was considered worthwhile. Sur-

prisingly, very little structural modification was required to support the new engine pods, a tribute to how strong the basic B-36 was. Additional oil tanks were installed in the outer wing panels to hold the special oil the jet engines required. Controls for the jet engines were mounted on a separate panel above the pilots' heads, while instrumentation was provided on two subpanels mounted below the main instrument panel in front of the pilots. Surprisingly, the flight engineer was not provided with any jet instrumentation or controls other than some fire warning lights.

The B-36D was supposed to use an improved K-3A bombing and navi-

gation system. But like many things, development problems prevented the K-3A from being delivered in time to equip the first B-36Ds, which used a K-1 unit that was little more than a refined version of the APQ-24 used in the B-36B. All aircraft were eventually retrofitted with the K-3A. An AN/APG-32 gun-laying radar replaced the APG-3 to direct the tail turret. The B-36D was fitted with "snap-action" bomb-bay doors that could open and close in only two seconds, minimizing the drag penalty usually associated with getting ready to drop bombs over the target. The doors were hydraulically actuated and proved to be more reliable than the earlier sliding doors. Take-off and landing weights were up to

The B-36 assembly line turned out an average of one aircraft per week for most of the production run. Here aircraft still do not have their outer wing panels and are proceeding straight down the line instead of being angled. (Lockheed Martin)

Two pairs of J47 turbojet engines were introduced on the B-36D, and would be a feature of all subsequent production models. The engine pod itself was essentially identical to the one used on the Boeing B-47 although the outrigger landing gear was deleted. Since the engines were not intended to be used all the time, special aerodynamic covers were designed that closed-off the air intakes when the engines were not in use. The intakes are shown open at above left and closed in the photo below. The

photo above right shows the original J35 installation used on a B-36B to demonstrate the concept. Note that the bottom of the pod is not sculptured and there is no sway brace between the pylon and the wing. (Convair via the San Diego Aerospace Museum)

370,000 and 357,000 pounds, respectively. Another major improvement was that all of the flying surfaces were now covered with metal skin instead of doped fabric.

The nomenclature for the B-36D's 15 crewmembers changed slightly: aircraft commander, two pilots, two engineers, navigator, bombardier, two radio operators, and an observer forward; and five gunners aft. In reality, one of the radiomen operated the ECM equipment, the other operated the nose turret, while one of the pilots and the observer operated the forward upper gun turrets.

The modification of a single B-36B (44-92057) to demonstrate the jet engines was authorized on 4 January 1949, and the aircraft made its first flight on 26 March 1949. Due to the unavailability of production engines, it had four Allison J35 engines in the pods in place of the

later J47s. The only external differences were that this installation did not include a sway-brace that was used on production examples to correct a slight vibration problem and that the underside of the nacelles were not "sculpted" like the B-47. This aircraft was not a prototype D-model as is often reported – it incorporated none of the other features of the new aircraft such as the snap-action bomb bay doors. A second B-36B (44-92046) was also used during the J47 test program.

The last 11 B-36Bs were equipped with jet engines on the assembly line, becoming B/RB-36Ds prior to delivery. The first new-build B-36D flew on 11 July 1949. The first B-36D was accepted by the Air Force in August 1950 and sent to Eglin AFB for testing. By June 1951, 26 B-36Ds had been delivered, and the last of 76 B-36Ds was accepted in August 1951.[3]

A decision was made to add the engines to all existing B-36As and B-36Bs (becoming RB-36Es and

B-36Ds). The Fort Worth plant was already overcrowded building the B-36, so after the first four B-36Bs (44-92026, 034, 053, and 054) were converted, the modification effort was transferred to San Diego. Each aircraft was completely overhauled, and new control surfaces, jet engines, and the "snap-action" bomb bay doors were added. The first B-36B (44-92043) to be converted arrived at San Diego on 6 April 1950, and was redelivered to the Air Force in November. The last (44-92081) was delivered to the Air Force on 14 February 1952. All B-36B conversions resulted in B-36Ds – there were no converted RB-36Ds.

The performance benefit was significant. Although originally the Air Force claimed the new engines boosted the top speed to 439 mph at 32,120 feet and the service ceiling to 45,020 feet, this was later revised to 406 mph at 36,200 feet and a service ceiling of 43,800 feet. Whether this slight discrepancy was due to mis-calculation, some overzealous public relations (the Congressional hearings were underway at the time), or changes in the aircraft themselves is not certain. The takeoff run was reduced by almost 2,000 feet.

Although still a great deal lower than the performance expected from the B-52, the B-36 was no longer considered a "sitting duck" and could outrun most contemporary fighters at altitude. (The speed quoted for an aircraft is usually at its best operating altitude – for contemporary fighters this was about 20,000 feet. The fighters generally lost several hundred mph by the time they got to 40,000 feet, if they could get there at all.)

At the end of 1951 the B-36's defensive armament system still remained operationally unsuitable. In fact, SAC viewed the "gunnery and defensive armament as the weakest link in the present B-36 capability." In April 1952 SAC ordered a series of gunnery missions known as FIRE AWAY to be completed by July. These showed that the performance of the B-36's defensive armament system was due in part to poor maintenance, and to inadequate gunnery crew training. This prompted TEST FIRE, a three month exercise that began in September 1952.

As anticipated, TEST FIRE confirmed the overall conclusion of FIRE AWAY that the performance of the B-36's defensive armament was nearly as bad as ever. Because of this, HIT MORE was launched in early 1953 to pool the efforts of the Air Force, General Electric, and Convair to finally devise an effective defensive system. The HIT MORE results were encouraging, and proved that the B-36's defensive armament could be made to work well after numerous but minor modifications. More effective training of the gunners and maintenance personnel was the final link in obtaining a truly operational system.

An RB-36H on the maintenance line at Convair in Fort Worth. A wide variety of tail markings from different bomb wings are visible on aircraft in the background. All B-36s came home to Fort Worth several times during their careers for maintenance and modifications. SAM-SAC was among the first programs in the Air Force where the original manufacturer was largely responsible for the depot-level maintenance of a weapons system. Note the tail radar on the RB-36H is exposed as the ground crew works on it. (Lockheed Martin)

RB-36D

General LeMay strongly influenced the decision to produce a reconnaissance version of the B-36. LeMay had observed first-hand the lack of reconnaissance capability against Japan during World War II. One of his first actions upon taking command of SAC was to insist on an up-to-date supply of strategic reconnaissance aircraft. LeMay ordered the largely non-combat-capable B-36As were remanufactured into strategic reconnaissance aircraft under the RB-36E designation while Convair began to manufacture new-build RB-36Ds.

The RB-36D was a specialized photographic-reconnaissance was generally similar to the bomber version, but carried a crew of 22 to operate and maintain the photographic reconnaissance equipment. The are that normally housed the forward (No. 1) bomb bay was modified into a pressurized compartment that contained 14 K-17C, K-22A, K-38, and K-40 cameras, including one with a 48-inch focal length lens. Bomb bay No. 2 carried 80 T86 flash bombs, and bomb bay No. 3 contained an auxiliary fuel tank. The area that normally contained bomb bay No. 4 was used instead to carry ferret elec-

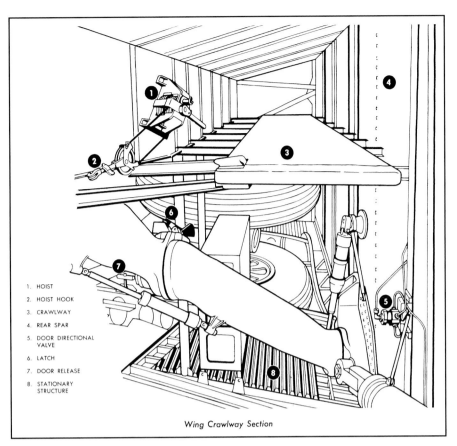

1. HOIST
2. HOIST HOOK
3. CRAWLWAY
4. REAR SPAR
5. DOOR DIRECTIONAL VALVE
6. LATCH
7. DOOR RELEASE
8. STATIONARY STRUCTURE

Wing Crawlway Section

At the fuselage junction, the B-36 wing was over 7.5 feet thick. A crawlway inside the wing allowed crewmembers to perform minor maintenance on the landing gear and R-4360 engines while the aircraft was in flight. This crawlway was not pressurized, and the conditions inside the wing were extremely cold at high altitude. The crew wore exposure suits and carried oxygen, but working in this environment for even short periods of time was not pleasant. (U.S. Air Force)

tronic countermeasures (FECM) equipment. Three large radomes were mounted on the bottom of the fuselage under this area. Convair took this opportunity to lighten the structure around this area since it no longer had to carry bombs. Later, the FECM equipment would be moved

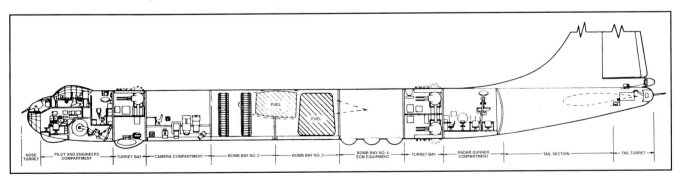

The RB-36D was representative of all the RB-36 models, with a camera compartment located in the bomb bay No. 1 location, flash bombs in bomb bay No. 2, fuel in bomb bay No.3, and ferret ECM equipment in the area where bomb bay No. 4 should have been. Later the electronic equipment would be moved to the aft fuselage to allow bomb bay No. 4 to be activated to carry nuclear weapons. (U.S. Air Force)

of months, and the first seven RB-36Ds came off the production line before any bomber-versions of the jet-augmented design. All of the 24 RB-36Ds were "new-build" aircraft although the first seven had originally been ordered as B-36Bs and were modified on the production line before being delivered as RB-36Ds. All were delivered to the 28th Strategic Reconnaissance Group at Rapid City AFB, North Dakota (now Ellsworth AFB) between June 1950 and May 1951.

The weather at the northern bases could be horrible. Here a B-36D takes-off from Eielson AFB near Fairbanks during the joint Army-Air Force Alaskan Theater winter maneuvers on 15 February 1954. Code named Operation NORTH STAR, temperatures as low as –40 degF hampered maintenance but did not prevent the success of the air operation. (San Diego Aerospace Museum Collection)

within the aft fuselage and the three radomes would be moved about 20 feet aft, freeing up the fourth bomb bay to carry nuclear weapons. Reactivating the bomb bay, accomplished under a later phase of Project ON TOP, as fairly involved since two bulkheads and numerous other structural elements had to be beefed up to support the weapons load. At the same time, the other two bomb

bays (Nos. 2 and 3) were equipped to carry a range of weapons. The normal defensive armament of sixteen 20-mm cannon was retained.

The first RB-36D (44-92088) made its maiden flight on 18 December 1949, only six months after the jet demonstrator had flown. The RB-36D actually preceded the B-36D into service with SAC by a couple

The longest known B-36 flight was made by a Convair test crew flying an RB-36D (44-92090). The aircraft took off at 09:05 on 14 January 1951, and landed at 12:35 on 16 January – exactly 51.5 hours in the air. Although this flight was unusual, most B-36 flights lasted more than 10 hours, and it was not unusual for missions to last 30 hours. The average training mission was scheduled for 24 hours.

The first RB-36D (44-92088) was modified to carry a "Boston Camera" with a 240-inch focal length lens. Even the B-36 could not actual-

This is what the majority of the B-36 fleet looked like towards the end of their service careers. This B-36H does not yet have the large U.S. AIR FORCE markings on the forward fuselage, but it has been sprayed with the white "high altitude camouflage" on the undersides of the wings and fuselage. (Lockheed Martin)

ly carry a camera over 20 feet long, so the lens used a set of mirrors to achieve the 240-inch effective length. Each negative measured 18x36 inches and the camera was reportedly able to photograph a golf ball from 45,000 feet. A large circular opening was cut into the left side of the fuselage and the camera was installed in the normal camera compartment. The camera was tested for about a year prior to being removed from the RB-36D in 1955 and installed in a C-97. This RB-36D was never used operationally, and the camera was eventually donated to the Air Force Museum in 1964.

RB-36E

In an effort to quickly gain an intercontinental reconnaissance capability, Gen. LeMay ordered the B-36A fleet remanufactured into RB-36Es that were substantially similar to the upcoming RB-36D. Since the YB-36A (the first B-36A) was going to be destroyed during structural testing, the original YB-36 (42-13571) was also modified to RB-36E standard to give the Air Force 22 aircraft.

The remanufacturing effort was much more involved than is normally reported. After the aircraft arrived back at Convair, they were stripped of all equipment, which was returned to the vendor or depot for maintenance and upgrading. The airframes were then stored on the flight line for a few months while special jigs were built. Eventually, each airframe was broken down into its major components – forward fuselage, mid fuselage, wings, etc. These components were cleaned and brought up to production standards, then reintroduced onto the normal production line. Each RB-36E then proceeded down the line for a second time. For unexplained reasons,

The B-36As (and YB-36) were broken down into their major components outside Building No. 4 in Fort Worth. The components were refurbished and reintroduced onto the assembly line (below). The airframes then proceeded down the line a second time and emerged as newly-remanufactured RB-36Es. (Lockheed Martin)

there was a single exception to this – one aircraft (44-92008) went through the remanufacturing process in the open air on the ramp next to Building 4. (The aircraft was neither the first nor the last to be remanufactured, so there appears to be no rationale.)

The R-4360-25 engines were replaced by R-4360-41s, and the aircraft were also equipped with the four J47 jet engines. The same reconnaissance cameras and electronic systems scheduled for the RB-36D were used. The aircraft were also fitted with the 20-mm defensive armament that had not been ready when they were initially built, and they also received the new "snap action" bomb bay doors used on the B-36Ds. The last aircraft was completed in July 1951. Like the RB-36D, the RB-36E was designed for all-purpose strategic

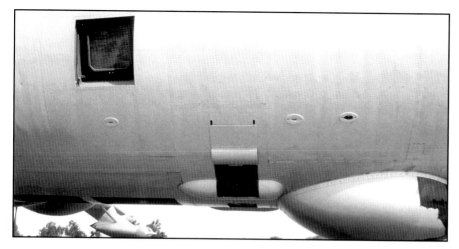

reconnaissance, day-and-night mapping and charting, as well as bomb damage assessment missions.

B-36F

The B-36F differed from the B-36D primarily in having more powerful 3,800-hp R-4360-53 engines, boosting the top speed to 417 mph, and the service ceiling rose to 44,000 feet. Late production aircraft (beginning with 50-1064) also had two A-7 dispensers (or one A-6 and one A-7) capable of dropping 1,400 pounds of chaff to confuse enemy radars. There were very few other changes, mainly just minor rearrangement of some cabin equipment.

The first B-36F made its maiden flight on 18 November 1950, and was accepted by the Air Force in March 1951. The first B-36F did not reach SAC until August 1951, the aircraft having been used for continued testing up until that time.[4]

At first, the R-4360-53 engines of the B-36F were not entirely satisfactory because of excessive torque pressure as well as ground air cooling and

The RB-36-series of aircraft had a wide variety of cameras. Each side of the fuselage (top and above) had two camera ports. Underneath the fuselage also had two large camera ports, each with multiple cameras (below). All the camera ports were covered by doors when not being used. These photos are of the RB-36H (51-13730) preserved at Castle AFB, California. (Dennis R. Jenkins)

The different areas using aluminum skin (shiny) and magnesium skin (dull) are readily apparent on this RB-36D (49-2688) during its acceptance flight. The RB-36s used aluminum to cover the new pressurized camera compartment where the bomber versions used magnesium to cover bomb bay No. 1. (Convair via the San Diego Aerospace Museum).

combustion problems. However, these problems were resolved fairly quickly, and the new engines proved to be quite reliable in service.

RB-36F

The Air Force ordered 24 RB-36F long-range reconnaissance versions of the B-36F. The first four RB-36Fs were accepted in May 1951, with the last being delivered in December 1951. The reconnaissance

A very confusing airplane. This is the first B-36B-1-CF (44-92026) that was subsequently converted to a B-36D-10-CF. However this photo shows the aircraft with a full complement of RB-36 radomes under the nose and bomb bay No. 4 and no guns installed in the nose turret. The fuselage skin around bomb bay No. 1 is still the dull magnesium, indicating that the area has not been converted into a pressurized compartment. The official lists indicate this aircraft was used for "propeller vibration tests" between the time it was completed and the time it was the first aircraft converted to a D-model at Fort Worth – it does not appear to have been delivered to the Air Force as a B-model. It was also, apparently, used to test at least the aerodynamic portions of the reconnaissance variant. This photo has often been identified as depicting the "first RB-36D" and used to justify a claim that the first RB-36D made its initial flights without jet pods. In fact, the first RB-36D had jet pods on its first flight, and this aircraft has no association with that event. (San Diego Aerospace Museum Collection)

Other than the addition of the jet engine pods, there was little external difference between the late production B-36s and the earlier B-36A and B-36B. There was also virtually no external difference between the various late production variants – essentially you had to look at the serial number to differentiate the models. The "bumps" on the upper wing surface near the fuselage were added to accommodate the four-wheel main landing gear. (San Diego Aerospace Museum Collection).

Convair workmen apply the "high altitude camouflage" paint to the bottom of the B-36 fuselage. Very little was masked off, and most of the line was "fuzzy" as a result. The first few aircraft were painted in the Experimental Building, but most were sprayed in the open air on the ramp. (Lockheed Martin)

equipment in the aircraft was generally similar to the RB-36D.

On 16 June 1954, SAC's four RB-36-equipped heavy strategic reconnaissance wings were given a primary mission of strategic bombing with reconnaissance becoming a secondary mission. On 1 October 1955, the RB-36 reconnaissance wings were redesignated heavy bombardment wings, while retaining a latent reconnaissance capability. To better accommodate the change in missions, the RB-36s had their FECM equipment moved from bomb bay No. 4 to locations in the aft fuselage. THis allowed bomb bay No. 4 to be rebuilt to accommodate nuclear weapons. As part of later phases of Project ON TOP, bomb bays No. 2 and No. 3 were also reconfigured to increase their weapons-carrying abilities.

B-36G

The B-36G was the designation initially applied to a swept-wing, jet-powered version of the B-36F. Two B-36Fs (49-2676 and 49-2684) were ordered converted to B-36Gs, but the designation was changed to YB-60 before they were completed. See Chapter 6 for more details.

B-36H

The B-36H was the major production version of the B-36, with a total of 83 being built. The B-36H was much the same as the B-36F, but relocated the K-system electronic components to pressurized compartment to facilitate in-flight maintenance, and featured a rearranged flight deck with a second flight engineer. A new AN/APG-41A gun-laying radar used twin tail radomes, and was essentially two APG-32s, allowing one radar to track an immediate threat while the second continued to scan for other threats.

The engines were six R-4630-53s and four J47-GE-19s, the same as the B-36F. Slightly improved ECM equipment was included, as were the chaff dispensers introduced on late B-36Fs.

The B-36H was flown for the first time on 5 April 1952, although deliveries did not begin until December 1952. One of the reasons deliveries were held up was that an RB-36F had suffered a pressure bulkhead failure while flying at 33,000 feet. The accident was traced to a defec-

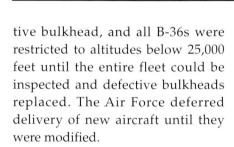

This was the view from a rear gunner's position on the B-36. The pilot also relied on the gunners to observe the engines for smoke and oil leaks. (Max Campbell)

tive bulkhead, and all B-36s were restricted to altitudes below 25,000 feet until the entire fleet could be inspected and defective bulkheads replaced. The Air Force deferred delivery of new aircraft until they were modified.

Due to an intermittent vibration, the B-36's original propeller blades carried flight restrictions that hampered performance. Convair and the Air Force had investigated different propellers (usually 16-foot diameter four-bladed units) even before the XB-36 was rolled out, but despite repeated flight tests using a variety of B-36s, a satisfactory arrangement could never be found. Instead. new blade, made by a special flash-welding process, was developed for the existing propellers could be used freely except for landing and takeoff.

This blade weighed an extra 20 pounds (1,170 pounds each), but its greater efficiency promised to compensate for the loss in aircraft range. The first of 1,175 of the new blades were installed on the B-36H, although they were later retrofitted to most of the fleet.

RB-36H

The Air Force bought 73 long-range reconnaissance versions of the B-36H. The camera and ECM/ferret equipment was generally similar to

the earlier RB-36s, while all other systems were identical to the standard B-36H.

B-36J

The B-36J was the final production version of the B-36. It had two additional fuel tanks, one in each outer wing panel, which increased the fuel load by 2,770 gallons. The aircraft also had a stronger landing gear which permitted a gross takeoff weight of 410,000 pounds. The only external change was a single elongated radome to cover the twin antennas of the APG-41A gun-laying radar in the tail, a change that had been introduced during B-36H production.

The first B-36J made its maiden flight in July 1953. The last 14 of the 33 B-36Js were completed as Featherweight III aircraft, with the last being delivered to the Air Force on 14 August 1954. These were the only Featherweight aircraft to be completed as such on the production line (others were modified after production). The reduction in weight enabled a service ceiling of 47,000 feet to be reached, although some missions were flown over 50,000 feet. Featherweights cost approximately $100,000 less, mainly because they did not carry the 20-mm cannon or turrets.[5] Later B-36Js were delivered with new "high altitude camouflage" white paint protecting sensitive areas of the lower wing and fuselage. The same "anti-flash" paint scheme, meant to protect from the heat flash from a near-by atomic weapon detonation, was subsequently applied to most (perhaps all) other B-36s.

By the time the last J-models were being delivered, the entire B-36 fleet showed marked reliability improvements, largely because of Project SAM-SAC. This program, initiated in 1953, required the cyclic reconditioning of all operational B-36s (215 as of September 1954) and constantly tied up 25 aircraft in depots. The intensive maintenance paid off for both the older B-36s and the latest and final B-36Js. In the same vein, the crew-to-aircraft ratio (too low for many years) began to improve as the number of combat-ready crews grew steadily.

The pilot's stations on the B-36D. Note the jet controls on the overhead panel – a convenient place to locate them that did not require rearranging the main instrument panels. The jet engine instrumentation was located on two subpanels located below the main instrument panel near the center pedestal. (Lockheed Martin)

The B-36 was certainly outmoded by mid-1955, but it had served well as SAC's primary atomic bomb carrier and perhaps the major deterrent to Soviet aggression. Meanwhile, the Air Force found ways to keep enhancing its effectiveness. The Quick Engine Change Program combined an engine and accessories in a power package that could be quickly installed in the field. Applied to other aircraft as well, the change program for B-36s ran from 1953 until September 1957.

The B-36 was scheduled to be replaced by B-52s, and beginning in February 1956, B-36s were flown to Davis-Monthan AFB where the Mar-Pak Corporation handled their reclamation. However, defense cutbacks in FY58 slowed the B-52 procurement

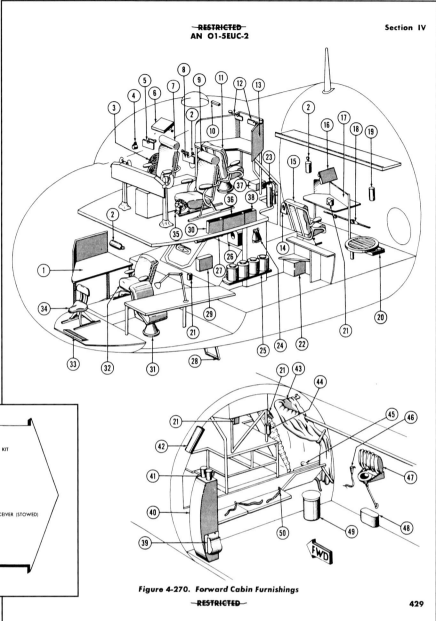

1. RADAR-BOMBARDIER'S TABLE
2. PORTABLE OXYGEN BOTTLE
3. CABIN VENT FAN STOWAGE
4. COMPASS
5. COPILOT'S SUN VISOR
6. JET CONTROL PANEL
7. COPILOT'S SEAT
8. PILOT'S SUN VISOR
9. PILOT'S SEAT
10. ASTRODOME PANEL
11. FLIGHT ENGINEER'S SEAT
12. FLIGHT ENGINEER'S SUN VISOR
13. FLIGHT ENGINEER'S TABLE
14. RADIO COMPARTMENT HEATER
15. RADIO OPERATOR'S SEAT
16. EMERGENCY HAND AXE AND KNIFE
17. RADIO OPERATOR'S TABLE
18. ASTRO COMPASS BAR (STOWED)
19. CUP DISPENSER
20. SCANNING STATION
21. FIRST AID KIT
22. SEXTANT STOWAGE
23. 4-TB FIRE EXTINGUISHER
24. PARACHUTE STATIC LINE
25. INSULATED LIQUID CONTAINERS

26. NOSE COMPARTMENT HEATER
27. MAP TUBE
28. ENTRANCE LADDER
29. BLOOD PLASMA & BATTLE SPLINT KIT
30. MAP CASE
31. NAVIGATOR'S SEAT
32. RADAR-BOMBARDIER'S SEAT
33. SPOTTING SIGHT KNEE PAD
34. NOSE GUNNER'S SEAT
35. PILOT'S VENTILATING FAN
36. FLIGHT REPORTS
37. ASTRO COMPASS (STOWED)
38. ENGINEER'S DATA CASE
39. BLACKOUT CURTAIN (STOWED)
40. FOOD LOCKER
41. HOT CUPS
42. AN/CRC-7 TRANSMITTER AND RECEIVER (STOWED)
43. TOILET CURTAIN
44. A2 FIRE EXTINGUISHER
45. NOSE GUNNER'S LANDING SEAT
46. RELIEF TUBE
47. WASH BASIN AND WATER TANK
48. IGNITION TEST STOWAGE
49. TOILET
50. SAFETY BELT AND BENCH

RESTRICTED

Figure 4-270. Forward Cabin Furnishings
RESTRICTED   429

process, and caused the B-36 service life to be extended. Mar-Pak's contracts were put on hold, and components were salvaged from retired aircraft to keep the operational B-36s flying (since spare parts were no longer being produced). Further update work was undertaken by Convair at San Diego throughout 1957 to extend the life of the B-36s.

By December 1958, only 22 B-36Js remained in the operational invento-

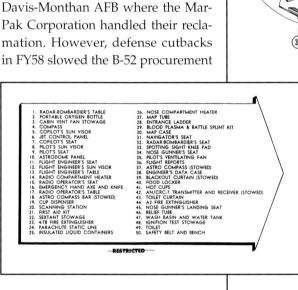

The forward crew cabin of the B-36D. Major changes would eventually include reconfiguring the flight deck on H- and J-models, moving the K-system electronics into the pressurized area, and installing – then removing – various items of crew comfort equipment. (U.S. Air Force)

ry. On 12 February 1959, the last B-36J (52-2827) left Biggs AFB, Texas, where it had been on duty with the 95th BW(H), and was flown to Amon Carter Field in Fort Worth, where it was put on permanent display. The

retirement of this B-36 marked the beginning of a new era – SAC became an all-jet bomber force on that day. Within two years, all but five B-36s which had been saved for museum display had been scrapped.

---

[1] Aviation Week, 28 January 1952, p 47. [2] Aviation Week, 12 September 1949, p 37. [3] Marcelle Size Knack, *Post-World War II Bombers*, Office of Air Force History, 1988, p 34. [4] *Ibid*, p 41. [5] *Ibid*, p 51.

This RB-36E (44-92020) was assigned to the 5th SRW at Travis AFB. This photo was taken near Travis AFB in August 1952. Note the location of two serials numbers on the tail. (Warren Bodie via Richard Freeman)

A B-36D from the 42nd BW in July 1955. Note that the cannon are missing from the tail turret. (Dave Menard Collection)

A B-36D (44-92065) assigned to the 326th BS/92nd BW, Fairchild AFB, Washington, in May 1955. Note the small piece of (unfortunately unreadable) nose art. (W. Balogn via the Norm Taylor Collection via Richard Freeman)

The extensive use of magnesium shows up well here – the dull areas are magnesium skin; the shiny areas are aluminum. The use of aluminum skin was primarily limited to pressurized areas where magnesium was inappropriate since it can not easily withstand pressure cycles. (Convair)

This RB-36E (44-92023) was assigned to the 5th SRW at Travis AFB. This photo was taken at Travis AFB in August 1952. Note the location of the serial number compared to the aircraft from the same unit on the top opposite page. (Warren Bodie via Richard Freeman)

The last B-36J takes off from Fort Worth on its maiden flight. The last 14 B-36Js were completed as Featherweight III aircraft without defensive armament. The "anti-flash" white paint on the lower fuselage and wings was designed to protect against the thermal flash of a nuclear explosion. (Lockheed Martin)

The first new-build B-36D (44-92095) was originally ordered as a B-36B, but was finished on the assembly line with jet engines and other improvements. (Convair via the San Diego Aerospace Museum)

A couple of B-36s meet their eventual replacement, the XB-52, at Edwards AFB. Although not discernable in this view, the RB-36D in the background was equipped with the Boston Camera. (Tony Landis Collection)

MAGNESIUM OVERCAST

Like most aircraft of the early Cold War, the B-36 served its early career in natural metal finish. In the B-36's case, this meant a combination of dull magnesium and shiny aluminum. Some early aircraft that were frequently deployed to bases in the Arctic had their wingtips and tails painted bright red – making it easier to find them if they were forced down in the hostile terrain.

There were some unit markings, but these were generally plain black – mainly triangles or circles on the tail in the old style bomber markings, and unit insignia on the nose. Occasionally a name made it onto the aircraft, but it could seldom be seen given the size of the fuselage.

The first YB-60 and the NB-36H had a little color in their markings, but neither made very many flights.

Late in their careers, the B-36 fleet received a "high altitude camouflage" (that's what Convair called it) consisting of "anti-flash" white on the bottom of the fuselage and wings. At the same time, most of the magnesium areas on most aircraft (there were always exceptions) were painted with an aluminized silver paint and the aluminum skin areas were painted with a clear acrylic in reduce corrosion.

Two B-36Hs also received a striking red, white, and blue paint scheme while they were being used to calibrate long-range optics on the Atlantic Missile Range at Cape Canaveral, Florida, during 1957. Unfortunately, few good photos of these truly unique-looking aircraft could be found.

A lot of bright red paint was used to cover the wingtips and tails of the handful of B-36As and B-36Bs that were routinely deployed to the northern bases. The red markings were intended to make it easier to spot the aircraft if they were forced down in the snow. (San Diego Aerospace Museum Collection)

The NB-36H atomic reactor test aircraft. At some point during its career it had the name "Crusader" in the blue strip on the nose. Note the radiation insignia on the vertical stabilizer. (Lockheed Martin)

A partially completed B-58 airframe was airlifted from Fort Worth to Wright Patterson AFB by using a B-36 in much the same manner as the FICON project. The B-58 was a structural test article. The inboard propellers were removed from the B-36, and the entire flight was conducted with the landing gear down since the B-58's wing would have interfered with its retraction. (Convair via Peter M. Bowers Collection)

WARBIRD**TECH**
SERIES

The Ton-Tom aircraft had a couple of spots of color. Note the blue wingtip pods that housed the docking mechanisms, and the red test data boom on the nose. (Lockheed Martin)

The standard natural metal used by most of the B-36 fleet for most of its career. There was little to externally differentiate most B-36 models. (Tony Landis Collection)

The B-36J at the Air Force Museum before it was restored and placed inside the new museum building. (Peter M. Bowers)

The XB-36 was finished in overall dull silver with a standard World War II national insignia on the rear fuselage and a black serial number on the vertical stabilizer. (Convair via the San Diego Aerospace Museum)

The XC-99 used aluminum skin instead of the magnesium skin used on much of the B-36. A variety of small markings were applied to the vertical stabilizer over the years, and for a while a small XC-99 logo adorned the forward fuselage. Late in its career the top of the cockpit area was painted white. (Convair via the San Diego Aerospace Museum)

A marginal photo of an unusual Kirtland aircraft. This EB-36H (51-5726) was painted this way to assist in calibrating various optical sensors on the Atlantic Missile Range and elsewhere. Another EB-36H (52-1358) was similarly painted. (Courtesy of the Air Force Research Laboratory, Phillips Research Site History Office)

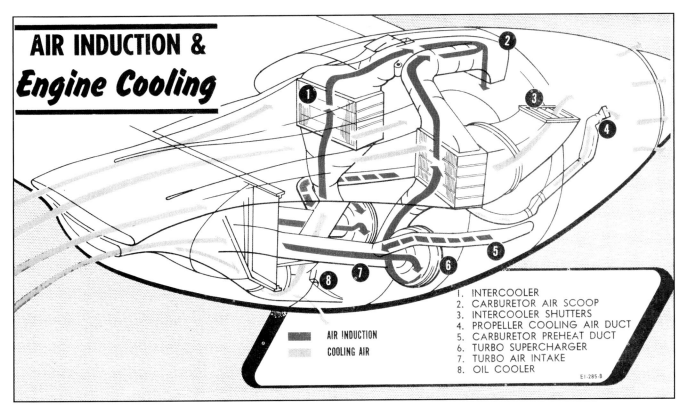

AIR INDUCTION & *Engine Cooling*

1. INTERCOOLER
2. CARBURETOR AIR SCOOP
3. INTERCOOLER SHUTTERS
4. PROPELLER COOLING AIR DUCT
5. CARBURETOR PREHEAT DUCT
6. TURBO SUPERCHARGER
7. TURBO AIR INTAKE
8. OIL COOLER

AIR INDUCTION
COOLING AIR

E1-285-B

The engine cooling diagram from the B-36 flight manual. Although Convair and the Air Force spent a great deal of time optimizing the nacelle configuration, engine cooling problems plagued the B-36's early career. (U.S. Air Force)

A rather fanciful paint scheme. The vertical and horizontal stabilizers are painted similar to the early arctic markings, except in yellow. The wing leading edges are also yellow, although surprisingly the jet cowlings are not. It appears that this scheme was never actually used, but similar art work was used by Convair San Diego in various logos, etc. during the SAM-SAC program. (Marty Isham Collection)

A group of red-tail B-36s along with at least one non-red tail aircraft. Note the variation in markings on the forward fuselage – some aircraft have buzz numbers, others do not. (San Diego Aerospace Museum Collection)

The end of the line. A B-36 arrives at the storage yard at Davis-Monthan AFB, Arizona, in January 1958. Unlike modern combat aircraft that frequently languish in the storage yard for years, most B-36s were reduced to metal ingots within a few months. (Frank Kleinwechter via Don Pyeatt)

The standard publicity photo handed out by General Dynamics during the 1970s. The airplane has been heavily (although well) retouched. (General Dynamics Corporation)

The B-36 was a popular attraction during open houses, shown here at Carswell on 20 May 1950. At this point there are no squadron color markings on the aircraft at all. (Frank Kleinwechter via Don Pyeatt)

Geometric tail codes were used by the Air Force during part of the B-36's career. The Triangle J code signified the 7th BW at Carswell AFB, Texas. During this period the numbered air force insignia (the 8th AF, in this case) was also painted on the tail, although the 15th AF painted it much further back. This photo was taken at Carswell AFB on 26 May 1950. (Frank Kleinwechter via Don Pyeatt)

A great photo of a red-tail B-model Unusually, the underside of the horizontal stabilizer is not painted red. (Lockheed Martin)

This B-36A shows the original bomb bay door configuration. The door on bays No. 1 and No. 4 slid up the left side of the fuselage; the doors for the middle two bays were split down the middle and slid up both sides of the fuselage since the wing would have gotten in their way otherwise.
(C. Graham via Dave Menard)

A Featherweight III airplane from the 11th BW at Carswell AFB in 1956. Note the flush blister cover and lack of a nose turret. Also notice that the bombardier's glazed panel is covered over, as it was on all aircraft equipped with a Y-3 periscopic bomb sight. (John Hoffman via Warren Thompson)

TECHNICAL 5 WONDERS

DEFENSIVE AND OFFENSIVE ARMAMENT

The 1950s were a time of wonder. Advances in material and the birth of mechanical and electromechanical computers had opened entirely new avenues of research. The pace of change, when compared to even 20 years earlier, was incredible. The B-36s used several very state-of-the-art systems.

DEFENSIVE ARMAMENT

The defensive armament installed on the B-36 represented the ultimate expression of the self-defense concepts that came into being during World War II. Although most later bombers (through the Douglas B-66) would continue to include tail armament, the B-36 was the last that made extensive use of turrets to provide complete hemispheric coverage. After investigating many different turret configurations, it was decided to use a variation of the remote control turret (RCT) that had found its first extensive use on the B-29 and A-26 during World War II. General Electric continued to develop the concept, and was selected to develop an improved system for the B-36.

The basic B-36 defensive armament consisted of eight remotely-controlled turrets, each equipped with two 20-mm cannon. The nose and tail turret were nonretractable and provided limited coverage directly ahead and behind the aircraft. Six other turrets were located in pairs on the upper forward fuselage, upper rear fuselage, and lower rear fuselage. These turrets all retracted into the fuselage and were covered by flush doors when not in use. The

turrets were designed to operate at altitudes up to 50,000 feet in temperatures between –50 degF and 122 degF.[1] Each turret was operated electrically from a gunner's sighting position located apart from the turret it controlled.

The basic RCT system was composed of one sight, one turret, one thyratron controller, a signal system, an input resolver, a computer, and various controls to monitor and activate the system. The upper and lower fuselage turrets also had retracting mechanisms. The entire system was very dependent upon a constant and well-regulated electrical supply, and this was one source of early problems. Since all movement of the turrets and cannon was based on the differential voltage between two signals, each signal had to start from a very precise baseline. The voltage regulators in the late 1940s were not truly up to the task, resulting in large errors in movement in early systems.

Unlike the sights in the B-29, which could be switched to control different turrets, each sight in the B-36 was dedicated to the turret closest to it. Four different types of sights were used on the B-36: yoke, pedestal, hemisphere, and tail.

The yoke sights were located in the four upper sighting blisters and controlled the upper turrets. The yoke

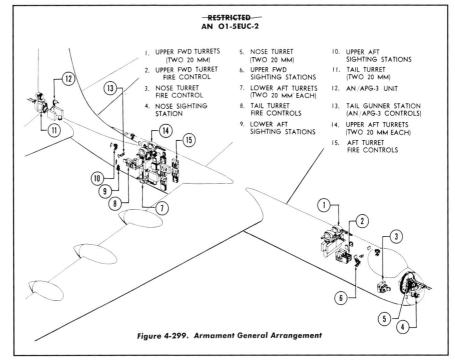

RESTRICTED
AN O1-5EUC-2

1. UPPER FWD TURRETS (TWO 20 MM)
2. UPPER FWD TURRET FIRE CONTROL
3. NOSE TURRET FIRE CONTROL
4. NOSE SIGHTING STATION
5. NOSE TURRET (TWO 20 MM)
6. UPPER FWD SIGHTING STATIONS
7. LOWER AFT TURRETS (TWO 20 MM EACH)
8. TAIL TURRET FIRE CONTROLS
9. LOWER AFT SIGHTING STATIONS
10. UPPER AFT SIGHTING STATIONS
11. TAIL TURRET (TWO 20 MM)
12. AN/APG-3 UNIT
13. TAIL GUNNER STATION (AN/APG-3 CONTROLS)
14. UPPER AFT TURRETS (TWO 20 MM EACH)
15. AFT TURRET FIRE CONTROLS

Figure 4-299. Armament General Arrangement

The remote-controlled turret system fitted to the B-36 was the most extensive defensive armament ever to equip an operational aircraft. This is a B-36B, but all models except the Featherweight IIIs were generally similar. (U.S. Air Force)

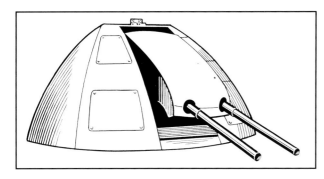

The nose turret was a late addition to the B-36 based on wartime experience. This forced a redesign of the entire nose section of all except the original XB-36. (U.S. Air Force)

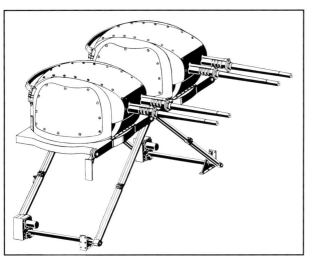

There were two sets of upper turrets located under sliding panels, one near the cockpit and one near the base of the vertical stabilizer. The turrets retracted by folding approximately 45° downward, hinged near the centerline of the aircraft. (U.S. Air Force)

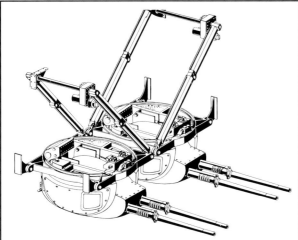

The lower turrets were generally similar to the upper turrets. Originally there were to have been two sets of lower turrets, but the APS-13 and APS-23 search radar was installed in the forward lower turret bay in all production B-36s. (U.S. Air Force)

ing fighter's wingspan with the target dimension knob and framing the target correctly, the gunner supplied the range of the attacking fighter to the computer. At the same time the gunner was expected to track the fighter accurately and smoothly, providing azimuth, elevation, and relative speed (relative angular velocity) to the computer.

The hemisphere sight controlled the nose turret and was offset to the right side of the nose, below the turret. The sight was a horizontally-mounted, double prism periscopic sight designed to give the gunner a full hemisphere of vision. The gunner, without changing his position, could see 90° to the right or left of straight ahead, as well as 90° up or down from 0° elevation. The eyepiece of the sight was fixed, and the gunner controlled the turret by manipulating control handles immediately below the sight. Since the sight protruded from the nose of the aircraft into the airstream, a desiccating system was provided to keep the prism free of moisture and a heating unit prevented frosting.

The hemisphere sight operated on much the same principle as the yoke and pedestal sights, except the gunner sighted through a single eyepiece with one eye. A dummy eyepiece blocked the unused eye, and could be rotated to accommodate either right or left eye-dominant gunners.

The tail sight was a radar set which was controlled by a gunner facing rearward in the aft compartment (some RB-36s shifted the gunner facing left on the port side of the aft cabin). The *SAC B-36 Gunnery Manual* boasted that "The gun-laying radar is highly developed and unbelievably accurate." Three different gun-laying radars were used; the

sight could be rotated in elevation from 90° above to 45° below horizontal, and in azimuth from 110° forward to 110° aft of broadside. The gunner tracked the target by manipulating the entire sight.

The pedestal sights were located in the lower blisters and controlled the lower turrets. The pedestal sight could be rotated in elevation from

45° above to 90° below horizontal, and in azimuth from 105° forward to 105° aft of broadside.

The yoke and pedestal sights had a small clear glass plate through which the gunner looked while aiming. When the sight was powered on, a view through the plate showed a center aiming dot surrounded by a circle of dots. By setting the attack-

WARBIRD**TECH**
S E R I E S

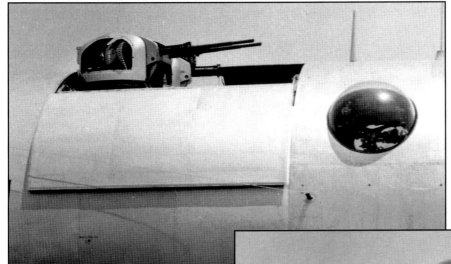

The upper forward turrets were located behind doors that slid down the outside of the fuselage to expose the turrets, creating a fair amount of drag in the process. (Peter M. Bowers)

The nose turret had limited travel, but could successfully defend from frontal attacks. The hemispheric sight is offset to the left in this photo. (U.S. Air Force via C. Roger Cripliver)

APG-3 in the B-36B was quickly replaced by the APG-32, while the APG-41 was used later. The early sets used a single antenna, while the APG-41 used two antennas above the tail turret, although in some later aircraft these were covered by a single elongated radome.

Each of the turrets was equipped with two M24E2 or M24A1 20-mm automatic cannon with a selectable rate of fire between 550 and 820 rounds per minute. Late in their careers the rate of fire was fixed at 700 rounds per minute for the tail

The APG-3 and APG-32 tail radar used a single radome, as shown on the B-36D at left. The later APG-41 used either two radomes (as shown on the B-36H at right) or a single elongated radome that covered both antennas. The tail turrets on later aircraft also differed in some details. (left: Peter M. Bowers; right: U.S. Air Force via C. Roger Cripliver)

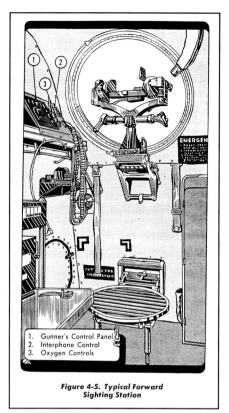

Figure 4-5. Typical Forward Sighting Station

1. Gunner's Control Panel
2. Interphone Control
3. Oxygen Controls

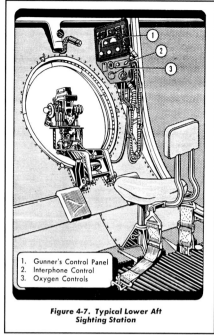

Figure 4-7. Typical Lower Aft Sighting Station

1. Gunner's Control Panel
2. Interphone Control
3. Oxygen Controls

Typical upper sighting station (right) and lower sighting station (above) on the B-36B. The later B-36 models were essentially identical. Each sight could be equipped with a camera that was used mainly for training purposes. (U.S. Air Force)

guns and 600 for all others. Each gun weighed 100 pounds, was 77.7 inches long (52.5 inches of this was the barrel), and had a muzzle velocity of 2,730 feet per second. The nose turret had 800 rounds (400 per box), while all other turrets had 1,200 rounds (600 per box). The ammunition was pulled out of an ammunition box by an ammunition booster mounted on the box (except for the lower turrets and some nose turrets) and fed through ammunition chutes to the gun feeders. The lower turrets used gravity to feed the ammunition.

Four different types of 20-mm ammunition were approved for use on the B-36: M97 high-explosive incendiary, M96 incendiary, AP1 armor-piercing incendiary, and AP-T armor-piercing with tracer. An M95 target practice round was also available, as was a "drill" round which could be used to practice loading and handling.

The retractable turrets were equipped with fire interrupters to prevent self-inflicted damage to the propellers, wings, or tail. The retractable turrets were also equipped with contour followers to prevent the guns from striking the aircraft, or pointing at parts of the aircraft housing personnel.

The upper and lower fuselage turrets were electrically retractable in order to reduce drag. Each turret was covered by a flush panel that slid down the outside of the fuselage when opened. Each turret could also be extended or retracted manually by means of a handcrank. The turrets were stowed in unpressurized compartments that could be entered in flight if required, and also served as a means of emergency escape during ground accidents (explaining why many photos show the turret doors open during taxi).

SAC determined that a three-ship "V" formation provided the maximum defensive firepower. In this formation, the aircraft in the lead trained all of its turrets forward (the

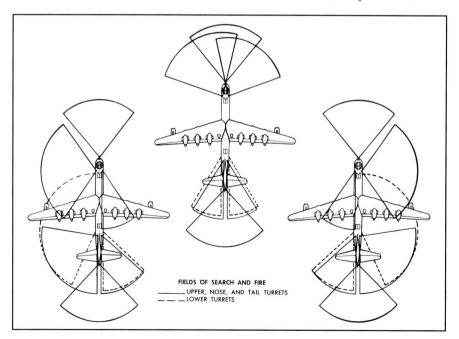

FIELDS OF SEARCH AND FIRE
——— UPPER, NOSE, AND TAIL TURRETS
- - - LOWER TURRETS

The HOME TOWN defensive fire formation. (U.S. Air Force)

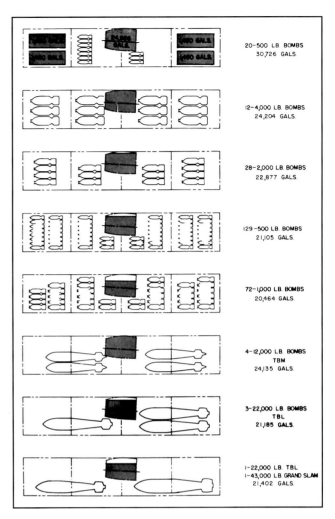

A turret from the Fort Worth B-36J restoration project. The aircraft at Fort Worth was manufactured as a Featherweight III, so it never was equipped with turrets. The restoration team nevertheless found one to display near the aircraft. (Aviation Heritage Association via Don Pyeatt)

The B-36 could carry bombs – lots of bombs. This drawing shows some of the possible conventional bomb and fuel configurations available to the B-36D. Unclassified handbooks and manuals of the era did not list nuclear weapons. (U.S. Air Force)

lower and upper aft turrets swiveled completely forward and provided upward and downward coverage). The aircraft on each side trained all of its turrets to that side. The exception, of course, was the tail turret that always faced aft. This plan left no area covered by less than two turrets (four cannon), and simplified coordination between the gunners. This formation was called HOME TOWN, and was the standard attack formation at altitudes under 35,000 feet.

Above 35,000 feet the importance of beam attacks was lessened since very few contemporary fighters could actually keep up with the B-36 at high altitudes. Consequently, the HOME TOWN areas of search and fire were modified to provide more protection to the rear. This TAIL HEAVY formation primarily involved training the lower aft turrets of all aircraft to the rear (and downward). At these altitudes it was expected that most attacks would come from below and rearward, although there was a chance of a fighter climbing to altitude and waiting for the bombers directly ahead.

There were, of course, other formations and tactics available to the bomber crews. Pretty much all of them centered around the same three-ship "V" formation, but modified the search and fire areas for each of the turrets.

CONVENTIONAL BOMBS

Interestingly, the *SAC B-36 Gunnery Manual* contained a fairly large chapter on bombs and bombing equipment. This was because "as a gunner, you have duties and responsibilities not directly concerned with flexibly

A 43,000-pound bomb being loaded into the combined bomb bay 1/2. Note the sliding bomb bay doors towards the right of the photo. (Lockheed Martin)

gunnery ... you will assist [the bombardier] in the loading, fuzing, and arming of all bombs."

The B-36 was equipped with four large bomb bays. The B-36A and B-36B used electrically-controlled, cable-operated doors that slid in tracks up the side of the lower fuselage. The doors on bomb bays No. 1 and No. 4 were single-piece units that slid up the left side of the fuselage. The two middle bomb bays had doors split down the centerline and slid up both sides of the fuselage – the location of the wing prevented using a single-piece design. Each

door was 16.1 feet long. The doors were slow to operate, tended to stick in the extremely cold temperatures at 40,000 feet, and created undesirable drag at a time when speed was of the essence. Beginning with the B-36D, the aircraft were equipped with hydraulically-actuated "snap-action" doors that opened in approximately 2 seconds. There were two sets of 32.375-foot long doors on each bomber variant, one set covering the combined bomb bays Nos. 1 and 2, and the other set covering Nos. 3 and 4. The B-36B models were retrofitted with the new doors as they became B-36Ds.

Initially the RB-36s were not configured to carry bombs, only photo flash bombs in bomb bay No. 2 and an auxiliary fuel tank in bomb bay No. 3. Reconnaissance versions installed a pressurized compartment into the space previously used by bomb bay No. 1 that housed up to 14 cameras, a darkroom that allowed film cartridges to be reloaded, and the crew to operate and maintain the equipment. A special pallet that contained various ferret ECM equipment was carried in the area that was bomb bay No. 4 on the bombers, and was easily identified by the three large radomes protruding below the same area. Later this equipment was moved into the aft fuselage and the radomes were placed under the lower aft fuselage, allowing bomb bay No. 4 to be configured to carry a nuclear weapon. The bomb bay doors were also changed to more closely match the bomber models – Nos. 3 and 4 were covered by a single set of new 32.375-foot long doors, while bomb bay No. 2 was covered by a set of 16-foot doors that were modified from the original set of doors. Previously, bomb bays Nos. 2 and 3 had been covered by a single set of doors that were 33.66 feet long.

The B-36 was capable of carrying 67 different types of conventional, incendiary, cluster, and chemical bombs, as well as several types of mines. On the aircraft that had been modified to carry nuclear weapons, any airborne nuclear or thermonuclear weapon in the inventory could be carried. The B-36 was only aircraft that could do so. Only a single type of bomb could be carried in each bomb bay, although each bay could carry different types if necessary. The end bomb bays (Nos. 1 and 4) could carry a maximum of thirty-eight 500-pound bombs, nineteen

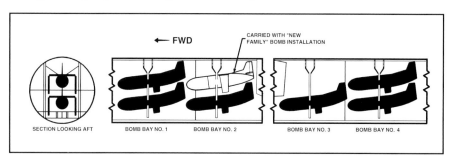

Convair and the Air Force also developed a decoy for the B-36 called the GAM-71 Buck Duck. Similar in concept to the Quail used on the B-52, the decoy was meant to distract enemy air defenses while the B-36 struck its target. Either 6 or 7 of the decoys could be carried by a single B-36. Although a few air-drop glide tests were conducted using a B-29, there are no records of a Buck Duck ever being carried by a B-36. The program was cancelled when it was decided to phase the B-36 out of service. (Lockheed Martin)

Convair provided two cargo carriers with each B-36. Loose items could be loaded into the carriers, which in turn could be loaded into the bomb bay. Up to six carriers could be carried at one time. (Lockheed Martin)

1,000-pound bombs, eight 2,000-pound bombs, or three 4,000-pound bombs. The two middle bomb bays (Nos. 2 and 3) were not as tall as the other two due to the wing carry-through structure, and could carry twenty-eight 500-pound bombs, sixteen 1,000-pound bombs, six 2,000-pound bombs, or three 4,000-pound bombs. Alternately, two 12,000-pound bombs, or a single 22,000-pound or 43,000-pound bomb could be carried in the combined bay 1/2 and bay 3/4. A portion of the separating bulkhead could be moved to accommodate the larger bombs.[2]

Bombs weighing up to 4,000 pounds each were carried on 15 different types of removable bomb racks. The racks were mounted vertically along the sides of the bomb bay in the traditional style. Larger bombs used special slings instead of conventional suspension lugs and shackles. The 22 B-36As were not equipped to carry the larger bombs when they left the factory, although they received that capability as part of a later phase of Project ON TOP after they were remanufactured into RB-36Es.

An early attempt at a precision-guided weapon was the Bell VB-13 Tarzon. This was essentially a British 12,000-pound "Tall Boy" bomb fitted with forward and rear shrouds with control surfaces that allowed the bomb to be guided to its target. The 21-foot-long, 54-inch-diameter, free-falling weapon was tracked visually by means of a colored flare in its tail and guided to its target via an ARW-38 radio link with the aircraft that dropped it. Development of the bomb had begun during World War II but had been halted when the war ended. The program was resurrected briefly in 1950, and 18 early B-36Bs (44-92045/92062) were equipped to carry two Tarzons each, although it is unclear how often the weapon was actually dropped from the aircraft. Interestingly, the provisions for carrying and controlling the bombs were retained when the aircraft were converted to B-36Ds. Although the bombs did not see action with the B-36, approximately 30 Tarzons were dropped from B-29s during the Korean conflict, with eight of them destroying or damaging the bridges they were aimed at.

The maximum 86,000-pound bomb load carried by later B-36s is the heaviest ever carried by an American bomber. Even the "big belly" B-52Ds used during Vietnam could only carry 60,000 pounds (twenty-four 750-pound and eighty-four 500-pound), while the B-1B only carries 42,000 pounds (eighty-four 500-pound) of bombs (although its theoretical load limit is 75,000 pounds). As a point of reference, one of the most respected interdiction aircraft in the current Air Force inventory is the F-15E Strike Eagle. Fully loaded, with a maximum fuel and weapon load, the F-15E weighs 86,000 pounds – the B-36 could carry that amount of bombs!

Bomb bay No. 3 could carry a 3,000-gallon auxiliary fuel tank in all aircraft, and bomb bay No. 2 could carry one in some aircraft.[3] Some sources report that all four bomb bays in some aircraft could carry these fuel tanks, but this could not be confirmed through official sources.[4] Early auxiliary fuel tanks were interesting in that they were basically metal frames with a sus-

One or more 3,000-gallon auxiliary fuel tanks could be loaded into the bomb bays to extend the range of the aircraft. (Convair via the San Diego Aerospace Museum)

pended fuel-proof "rubberized" canvas bag that contained the fuel.[5] The fuel cell was made by the Firestone Tire and Rubber Company. A later version of the fuel cell, manufactured by Goodyear, consisted of a rubber bladder inside a metal shell.

In a rather unique concept to assist the B-36 in deployments, both the ground power carts and a special cargo carrier were designed to be loaded into the bomb bays. Two cargo carriers were supplied by Convair with each aircraft, complete with wheels and tow bars to facilitate ground handling. Each cargo carrier could carry up to 14,000 pounds of loose items. Bomb bays Nos. 1 and 4 could each carry two of the cargo carriers, while the middle two bomb bays could each carry a single carrier.[6]

ATOMIC BOMBS

Interestingly, the B-36 was not designed to carry atomic bombs. But then, at the time no other bomber had been so designed either, and in 1946 only a few specially-modified B-29s were capable of carrying the new atomic devices. By the end of 1947, the Air Force had only 32 B-29s modified under Project SADDLE TREE available to carry atomic weapons. Many of these were described as "quite weary" after their wartime service, and all were assigned to the 509th Bombardment Group.

Part of the reason the Northrop flying wings did not garner more support within the Air Force was that the XB-35 had bomb bays too small to accommodate the 5-foot diameter, 10-foot long Mk III "Fat Man" or its Mk 4 replacement. The bombs had to be carried semisubmerged, resulting in a 6-percent loss in top speed and a 10 percent loss in combat range. The B-29 (and the B-50) had bomb bays that could only accommodate weapons shorter than 12 feet long, eliminating carriage of bombs such as the 15-foot long Mk 7.

Part of the problem during the late 1940s was that weapons developers would not tell the Air Force what the physical characteristics of their weapons were until they were in production, and then the data was highly classified. The designers provided "preliminary data" that was often substantially different from the weapon that finally emerged. This had been most evident on the North American B-45 program where the final weapon would not fit in the bomb bay of the light bomber. Modifications to aircraft bomb bays to accommodate atomic weapons was also considered "restricted" under the Atomic Energy Act of 1946. This was reiterated in May 1947 when the AEC stated "…any aircraft modification which would allow a reasonably accurate estimate of size, weight, or shape of the bomb … must continue to be Restricted

Data." This meant that you had to be cleared in order to simply look inside an empty bomb bay (many officials tried to enforce this restriction years after it had been officially lifted). The Air Force finally convinced the AEC that an empty bomb bay should be unclassified until the suspension lugs and sway braces were installed, since little information could be gained from the geometric shape of most bomb bays.[15]

The early nuclear weapons were designed without much regard to the aircraft that might carry it. Each bomb had a different center of gravity, sometimes radically different shapes, and required different suspension equipment and sway braces. This greatly complicated the design of aircraft bomb bays. The problem is

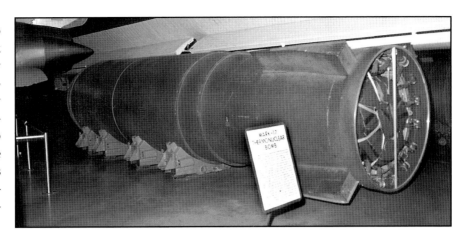

The largest thermonuclear weapon ever deployed by the United States was the Mk 17 (TX-17). (Terry Panopalis)

exemplified by the situation surrounding the Mk 6 weapon. As early as August 1949 the Air Force had requested that Sandia Laboratory supply drawings of the weapon to allow the Air Force to begin planning

for its introduction to the inventory. Sandia refused, indicating they would turn over the data after the bomb design had been frozen for production (something that did not occur until mid-1951). The Air Force

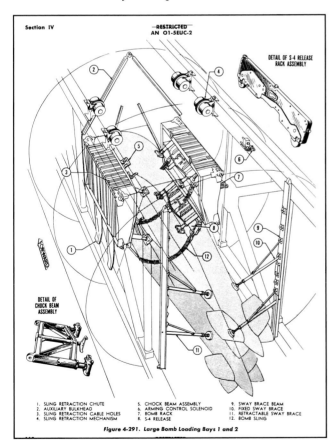

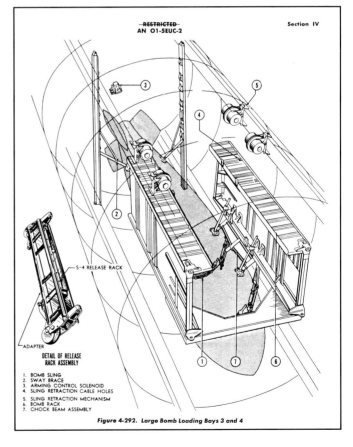

The size of the bomb bays in the B-36 allowed the aircraft to carry any bomb in the inventory. Large bombs were carried on slings suspended between bomb racks instead of the more traditional suspension lugs and shackles. Sway braces ensured the bombs did not move during flight. (U.S. Air Force)

commented that Sandia "consistently ignored our requirements and had used dimensions which required redesigning of handling, loading, and carrying equipment."

The B-36 was impacted less by these problems than most aircraft simply because it was essentially a large tube – a very large tube. In the end it could be modified relatively easily to carry almost any size or shape bomb the designers could dream up. It was the only aircraft ever capable of carrying the monstrous 25-foot long, 42,000 pound Mk 17 weapon.[16]

The components required to enable a bomber to carry early atomic weapons were relatively simple. A special bomb suspension system was installed, along with the appropriate sway braces and suspension lugs. Electronic "T-boxes" controlled, tested, and monitored the bomb during flight, while arming controls and a method to insert the "capsule" that allowed the bomb to go critical were also required.

Concurrently with the weapons programs, Project GEM (global electronics modernization) provided world-wide navigation equipment and some cold weather modifications that allowed bombers to operate over and around the Arctic Circle. Project SADDLE TREE was the first effort to convert B-29s and B-36s to carry the Mk III "Fat Man" type atomic bomb, the weapon being produced immediately after the war. Primarily this involved installing the appropriate suspension equipment and the T-Boxes. Between May 1947 and June 1948 the first 18 B-36Bs were modified to the SADDLE TREE configuration while the last 54 B-models were scheduled to come off the production line with most of the changes already in place. By the end of 1950 SAC had 52 B-36s equipped with the GEM/SADDLE TREE modifications, although at any given time many of these were out of service undergoing maintenance or being modified.[17]

In late December 1950, Project ON TOP began modifying additional aircraft, this time to carry the Mk 4, Mk 5, and Mk 6 devices. At the same time the Air Force began the development of the universal bomb suspension (UBS) system that could be easily reconfigured to accommodate atomic weapons 15–60 inches in diameter up to 128 inches long. The UBS was to be installed in B-29, B-36, B-47, B-50, and B-54 aircraft. When used aboard the B-36, the UBS could support Mk 4, Mk 5, Mk 6, Mk 8, and Mk 18 atomic bombs, and Mk 15, Mk 21, Mk 36, and Mk 39 thermonuclear weapons. The development of the UBS by North American Aviation was afforded the highest national priority available – even higher than the ongoing police action in Korea. All of these modifications resulted in the B-36 being able to carry a single nuclear weapon in bomb bay No. 1 where it was most convenient for crew members to arm the weapon.[18]

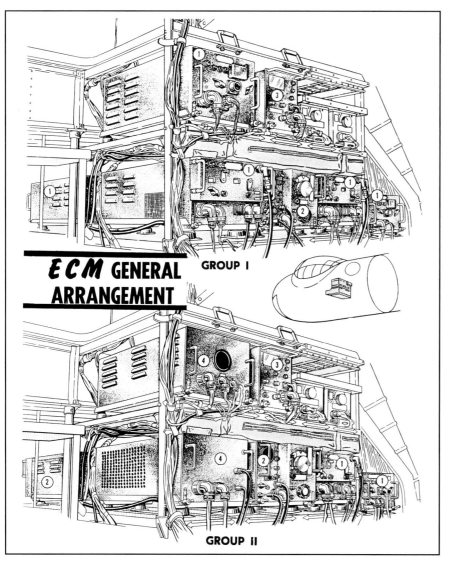

The Group I and II ECM equipment from a B-36H Featherweight III. (U.S. Air Force)

It was not until July 1950 that SAC decided that B-36s should be able to carry more than one atomic weapon at a time. No less than three separate configurations evolved from this requirement as part of later phases of ON TOP. At least 30 aircraft (12 B-36Ds and 18 B-36Hs) were modified to carry the UBS in all four bomb bays. Other aircraft were modified to carry the UBS in bomb bay No. 1 and another weapon in bomb bay No. 4. Some aircraft could reportedly carry multiple weapons of the same type in a single bomb bay. Beginning in 1952 the RB-36s (all models) were modified to carry nuclear weapons in bomb bay No. 4. The factory began to equip aircraft with the UBS beginning with the B-36F, and by the time the B-36H began to roll off the production line, they could carry the UBS in two bomb bays. It was a confusing time.

In 1951 a tentative configuration of the first hydrogen bomb was released to the Air Force – at six feet in diameter, 20 feet long, and weighing 50,000 pounds, only the B-36 was capable of carrying it. Project CAUCASIAN modified four B-36Hs to carry the TX-14 weapon as part of the test series.

As a result of the Operation CASTLE atmospheric tests, the TX-16 was cancelled on 2 April 1954 and the TX-14 and TX-17 were selected for production (called "stockpiled" by the AEC) as the Mk 14 and Mk 17, respectively. With the withdrawal of the TX-16, Project BAR ROOM was renamed CAUTERIZE. A high-priority program was undertaken to modify B-36s to carry production versions of the devices. By the end of 1953 there were 20 B-36s equipped to carry thermonuclear weapons; by the middle of 1955 there were 208 aircraft. CASTLE had demonstrated

the devices were capable of yielding the equivalent of 13.5 megatons, and the production Mk 17 yield was estimated at 20 megatons – the most powerful weapon ever deployed by the United States, and only deliverable by the B-36 (although the weapon would have physically fit inside the early B-52s; but had been retired before they showed up).

ELECTRONIC COUNTERMEASURES

One crucial advantage held by the B-36, and later the B-52, was that its size and load-carrying capacity gave it a great deal of room in which to incorporate new equipment. The first operational B-36s were equipped with essentially the same limited ECM equipment as contemporary B-29s. The radio operator served as the additional duty ECM operator, as in the B-29. During 1951, B-36s flew test missions at Eglin AFB to evaluate the effectiveness of the ECM and chaff systems, with results that indicated the B-36s could successfully penetrate existing radar defenses. Earlier

tests against Royal Air Force night fighters equipped with airborne intercept radars had proven ineffective against B-36Bs equipped with their standard ECM suite. The B-36's best defense was a combination of high altitude and ECM.

As most aircraft were delivered from Convair, they contained racks and antenna mounting locations for various ECM equipment. The aircraft maintenance manuals stated that "tactical organizations will supply and install the ECM equipment." Surprisingly, although the ECM equipment was not provided with the aircraft, the numerous antennas were, although they were stowed in plywood boxes in the aft compartment and one of the cargo carriers. The antennas were installed by whatever organization supplied the ECM equipment itself.[7]

Initially the ECM equipment for the bomber versions (the RB-36s carried more extensive ECM equipment) consisted of two configurations

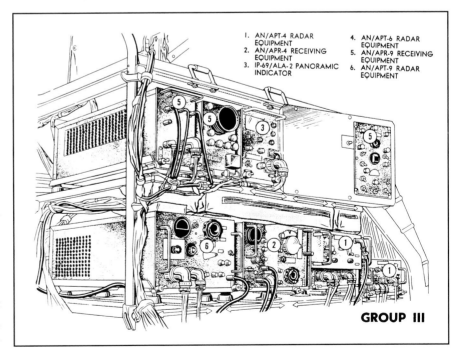

The Group III ECM equipment from a B-36H Featherweight III. (U.S. Air Force)

Convair technicians in a variety of colorful shirts work on R-4360s destined for installation in B-36s. (Convair via Don Pyeatt)

known as Group I and Group II, depending upon the frequency coverage desired. Group I consisted of two APT-4 transmitters that covered approximately 200–800 MHz (called megacycles at the time). Group II substituted an APT-1 transmitter for one of the APT-4s, extending coverage down to 90 MHz. In both cases a pair of APR-4 receivers were installed, covering approximately 40–1,000 MHz. This equipment would be significantly expanded on later bomber versions as electronic warfare became increasingly important. For instance, the APT-5A transmitter capable of covering 300–1,500 MHz was later added. By late 1954, a Group III had been developed that included the APR-4 and APT-4, an IP-69/ALA-2 panoramic receiver, APT-6 transmitter, APR-9 receiver, and APT-9 transmitter.[8]

The reconnaissance versions carried yet more ECM equipment, although some of it was actually "ferret" equipment designed to record and analyze enemy radio and radar transmissions. Most early RB-36s had three large radomes protruding from bomb bay No. 4, and a pallet in that bomb bay contained most of the electronic equipment. Control stations were installed in the aft compartment. A similar radome was fitted to the extreme forward fuselage immediately behind the glass nose. When SAC directed that the Featherweight RB-36s should have expanded bombing capabilities, the ECM/ferret equipment was relocated. The radomes were relocated to under the rear fuselage, and most of the electronic equipment was installed in the compartment previously used by the aft turrets. This allowed bomb bay No. 4 to be reconfigured to carry bombs.

On the GRB-36D FICON aircraft (and the lone JRB-36F), a single

APX-29A IFF/rendezvous set was installed. The antenna was located under a large radome on top of the forward fuselage, and proved to be one of the more recognizable features of the GRB-36D. The APX-29A allowed the RF-84K fighter to easily locate the waiting bomber when returning from a mission.

Late B-36Hs added an APS-54 radar warning receiver to tell the tail gunner or navigator if the aircraft was being illuminated by a surface or airborne radar. The APS-54 was a wide-band crystal video RWR that was effective from 2.6–11 GHz. The system provided limited azimuth data – basically indicating if the threat was ahead-of or behind the B-36. One problem was that the APS-54 could be easily damaged if it was illuminated by the APS-23 search radar of a nearby B-36. This was the first "modern" RWR to enter service with SAC, and quickly became standard equipment on most SAC bombers.

Modernization of the ECM equipment was a large part of the Featherweight program, and its $30,000,000 price tag included several significant equipment additions, such as the APS-54 radar warning receiver, two low frequency radar jammers, and a new APT-16 S-band jammer. The alterations also included the addition of another ECM operator position, so that there were individual crew positions for crew members operating low, intermediate, medium, and high frequency equipment. The manual A-7 chaff dispenser was replaced by the automatic ALE-7 dispenser on most aircraft.

[1] SAC Manual 50-30, *B-36 Gunnery*, November 1954. [2] AN 01-5EUB-1, *Flight Operating Instructions for the USAF Series B-36B Aircraft*, 16 November 1949, p 94. [3] *Ibid*, p 13. [4] Aviation Week, 12 September 1949, p 37. [5] AN 01-5EUC-2 (1B-36D-2), *Erection and Maintenance Instructions, USAF Series B-36D Aircraft*, 3 June 1954, p 637. [6] Aviation Week, 18 October 1948, p 12. [7] AN 01-5EUC-2 (1B-36D-2), *Erection and Maintenance Instructions, USAF Series B-36D Aircraft*, 3 June 1954, p 519. [8] 1B-36H(III)-1, *Flight Handbook for the USAF Series B-36H-III Aircraft*, 26 November 1954, p 229.

ODDS AND MODS

A HOST OF EXPERIMENTS

The 1950s were also a time of great experimentation. The Air Force was constantly exploring new technologies and new concepts to improve its war-fighting capability. The B-36 centered prominently in some of these experiments, several of which actually made it into operation.

FEATHERWEIGHTS

In February 1954 the Air Force approved the first of three phases of the Featherweight program to increase the operational altitude and range of the B-36. Phase I was a general weight reduction that simply deleted unnecessary items such as unused brackets, etc. All aircraft went through this "housekeeping." Phase II (also known as "Partial Featherweights") began to delete such things as crew comfort items, reduced some safety equipment, and minimized the number of spare parts and tools carried aboard the aircraft. This program was also applied across all types of B-36s, and the aircraft generally had a "-II" appended to their designation (i.e., B-36D-II).

The ultimate Featherweight was Phase III ("Full Featherweights"). Under this program all defensive armament except the tail turret and radar was deleted, and the forward and upper aft sighting blisters were deleted. The lower aft blisters were retained on most aircraft since they provided a convenient location for crewmembers to observe the engines for oil leaks, etc. On some aircraft these blisters were replaced by flat plexiglass, providing a small decrease in drag. Most of the remaining crew comfort equipment was also deleted. Without guns, the crew could be reduced, usually by two to five (remember that the forward gunners generally had other duties, such as navigating). These aircraft had a "-III" appended to their designations (sometimes written as "(III)" – B-36J-III or B-36J(III) – being equivalent).

The only known photo of "TANBO XIV," the tanker version of the B-36. Here the aircraft is undergoing "hydraulic tests" most likely related to its refueling equipment. Externally there was nothing to distinguish the aircraft from a normal B-36H. On the inside, the operator used the control panel at right to monitor the refueling. (Lockheed Martin)

The only known inflight photograph showing a RASCAL missile under a DB-36H. Note the retractable missile director under the rear fuselage. (Convair via Richard Freeman via the Jay Miller Collection)

The last 14 B-36Js were manufactured to the Featherweight III configuration, while many earlier aircraft of various models were converted in the field.

The modifications were successful. Not only did the third phase significantly improve the reliability of the aircraft since many troublesome components were removed (all the gunnery computers, sights, etc.), the maximum altitude of the aircraft was greatly increased. Officially the Featherweight IIIs could cruise at 47,000 feet, but missions as high as 51,000 feet were conducted.

TANBO XIV

As early as April 1948 both Convair and the Air Force had expressed interest in using the B-36 as a tanker to refuel the new jet-powered medi-

um bombers (B-47) being procured by the Air Force. A single B-36H (51-5706) was converted into an in-flight refueling tanker. Searching for a tanker that could refuel jet aircraft at higher altitudes and speeds, in early 1952 SAC became interested in a readily convertible B-36 bomber-tanker. The Air Force asked Convair to equip one B-36 with a probe and drogue refueling system for tests. The modification contract was approved in February 1952 and the work was completed in May. Test was satisfactory, even though it had to be postponed until the end of the month because of the late availability of the B-47 receiver aircraft. No other tests took place until January 1953, after an improved British-made probe and drogue refueling system was installed. The converted B-36H tanker had a crew of nine and could be returned to its stan-

dard bomber configuration in 12 hours. But the B-36's bomber commitments never allowed SAC to exploit these features.

DB-36H/RASCAL

Three B-36Hs (50-1085, 51-5706, and 51-5710)[1] were modified to carry the Bell GAM-63 RASCAL rocket-powered air-to-surface guided missile. RASCAL was an acronym which stood for RAdar SCAnning Link, named for the guidance system that was used during the missile's dive on the target. The GAM-63 was powered by a Bell-designed 4,000-pounds-thrust liquid-fueled rocket engine with three vertical in-line thrust chambers. The missile had a launch weight of 13,000 pounds and was 31 feet long with a body diameter of four feet. The missile could carry a 3,000-pound nuclear war-

head up to 100 miles at a speed of Mach 2.95. A retractable radio antenna was installed in the aft fuselage of the B-36 to provide an initial data link to the missile. The missile itself was carried semi-submerged in the combined bomb bay No. 3/4.

Originally, 11 other B-36Hs were scheduled to be modified as Rascal carriers under the designation DB-36H. However, in 1955 the Air Force decided that the B-47 was a more suitable carrier, and the DB-36 modification contract was cancelled. The majority of the test program took place during 1955, and all three aircraft had been scrapped by November 1957. The RASCAL turned out to be a fairly accurate and effective missile, but the concept rapidly became obsolete in the face of new developments in the field of air-launched missiles. The RASCAL program itself was cancelled on 9 September 1958.

XP-85 GOBLIN

The first jet fighters introduced near the end of World War II had insufficient range to escort the long-range B-35 and B-36 bombers then on the

The RASCAL missile was large, even for the B-36. The two photographs above show the first test fit of the missile attached to the DB-36H. Note the folding lower fin on the missile, and the plywood "security" fences around the aircraft. The vertical photo shows the launch platform from inside the bomb bay. The photo at right is the retractable missile guidance radar under the rear fuselage. (Lockheed Martin)

The little XP-85 Goblin was a unique design, especially in the days before computerized flight controls made inherently unstable aircraft a reality. The aircraft demanded more from its pilot than could reasonably be expected. (Peter M. Bowers Collection)

This XP-85 survives at the Air Force Museum, where it is displayed in front of the B-36. (Terry Panopalis)

drawing boards. As one possible solution to this problem, the Army Air Forces revived the parasite fighter idea of the early 1930s, and proposed that the long-range bombers carry their protective fighters right along with them. On 29 January 1944, the Army Air Forces invited the industry to submit concept proposals for parasite jet fighters.

The McDonnell Aircraft Corporation was the only company to respond, and proposed a small fighter aircraft to be carried partially inside a parent B-29, B-36, or B-35 heavy bomber. However, the AAF rejected this plan in January 1945, concluding that the fighter would have to be carried entirely inside the B-35 or B-36.

On 19 March 1945, McDonnell submitted a revised proposal for an even smaller aircraft with an egg-shaped fuselage, a triple vertical tail, a tailplane with pronounced anhedral, and vertically-folding swept-back wings. The engine was to be a 3,000-pounds-thrust Westinghouse J34-WE-7 axial-flow turbojet with a nose intake and a straight-through exhaust. The aircraft was to be fitted with a pressurized cockpit and an ejection seat. Armament was to be four 0.50-inch machine guns in the forward fuselage sides. It would be launched and recovered from a trapeze-like structure which would be extended from its parent aircraft.

The Army Air Forces liked the proposal, and ordered two XP-85 prototypes and a static test article on 9 October 1945. The Army Air Forces specified that the 24th (the first B-36B) and subsequent B-36s would be capable of carrying a single P-85 in addition to the usual bomb load. It was even planned that some B-36s would be modified so that

From the bottom looking up at the XP-85 mock-up tucked inside a B-36 bomb bay mockup. Note the folded wings and tight clearances all around. (Boeing)

The second series of FICON tests used the prototype YF-84F sweptwing Thunderstreak. The trapeze was much simpler than the one designed for the abortive XP-85 tests and proved much more effective. Of course, the more conventional handling qualities of the F-84 compared to the Goblin undoubtedly helped also. (Lockheed Martin)

they could carry three P-85 fighters and no bomb load. It appears that the first few B-36Bs actually had the mounting brackets for the trapeze included in their bomb bays.

Since the XP-85 was to be launched and recovered from a retractable trapeze underneath its parent bomber, no conventional landing gear was installed. A retractable hook was installed on top of the fuselage in front of the cockpit. During recovery, the XP-85 would approach its carrier bomber from underneath, and the hook would gently engage the trapeze. Once securely attached, the aircraft would be pulled up into the bomb bay. If an emergency landing were necessary, the aircraft was provided with a retractable steel skid underneath the fuselage, and the wingtips were protected by steel runners.

Since a B-36 could not be spared for the project, a B-29B (44-84111) was modified with a special launch-and-recovery trapeze for use in the initial testing. A few test flights were made with the XP-85, but the recovery operation proved to be much more difficult than expected, forcing several emergency landings using the retractable steel skid. The Air Force reluctantly concluded the Goblin was simply too difficult to handle and would probably be far beyond the capabilities of the average squadron pilot. In addition, it was projected that the performance of the XP-85 would likely be inferior to that of foreign interceptors that would soon enter service. Furthermore, a budget crunch in the autumn of 1949 led to a severe shortage of funds for developmental projects. Consequently, the Air Force terminated the XP-85 program on 24 October 1949.

FICON

The FICON (FIghter CONveyor) project was essentially a follow-on to the earlier XP-85 experiments. It was reasoned that many of the difficulties encountered with the XP-85 were due to that aircraft's unique shape, largely dictated by the requirement that it fit entirely into the bomb bay of a B-35 or B-36. If that requirement was relaxed, a more conventional fighter configuration could be used. Since the straight-wing Republic F-84 Thunderjet was proving to be fairly successful in service, an F-84E was chosen as the subject of the next round of experiments.

On 19 January 1951, Convair was authorized to modify an RB-36F (49-2707) to carry a modified F-84E. The bomb bay of the JRB-36F was

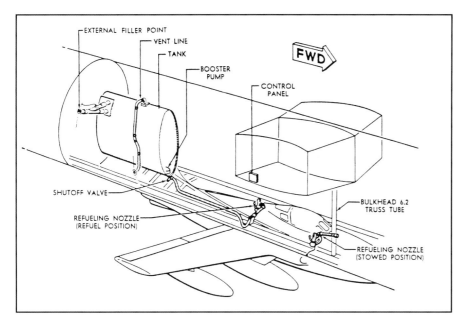

The JRB-36F/F-84E combination began its first tests on 8 January 1952 and the first complete cycle of retrieval, retraction, and launch took place on 23 April 1952. The tests were remarkably trouble-free, and demonstrated that a good pilot should have no particular difficulty performing the operation.

The RF-84K could be refueled from a special tank of JP-4 carried in bomb bay No. 4 – the B-36 did not normally carry jet fuel. (U.S. Air Force)

extensively modified, and the usual bomb racks were replaced by a retractable H-shaped cradle that was securely fastened to the rear wing spar. A single F-84E (49-2115) was modified to carry a hook on the upper nose ahead of its cockpit. During the recovery operation, the F-84E was to fly up underneath the B-36

and use its hook to engage a slot in the cradle. The cradle would then rotate down over the fuselage of the F-84E and engage hardpoints on the rear fuselage. Once attached, the F-84E would be pulled upward and nestle semi-submerged in the bomb bays of the JRB-36F. Launch was carried out by reversing this process.

By this time there was less emphasis on using the FICON concept for fighter escorts, but a new need had developed. Increasing Soviet air defenses were making it more difficult for the large strategic reconnaissance aircraft to penetrate Soviet airspace. The Air Force was not as worried about bomber penetration since by that time the two nations would be at war and fleets of bombers could assist in protecting each other. But reconnaissance aircraft penetrated one at a time, hopefully without being detected. The FICON concept offered a way to transport a relatively small reconnaissance aircraft close to Soviet borders. It could then be released, make its reconnaissance run, and return to the waiting carrier aircraft. The new Republic RF-84F Thunderflash would be perfect. And it could carry a small atomic weapon if the need ever arose.

A production RF-84K under a GRB-36D. Note the downward-canted horizontal stabilizers on the fighter to clear the sides of the bomb bay. Although the combination could take-off while mated, the fighter had to be released before the bomber could retract its landing gear. (Lockheed Martin)

In 1953, the first swept-wing YF-84F (51-1828) was modified in much the same manner as the F-84E, except that its horizontal stabilizer (which had been relocated in the sweptwing version) was sharply canted downward in order to clear the bottom of the B-36 during launch and recovery. Contracts awarded Convair and Republic in the fall of 1953 called for modifying 10 RB-36D-IIIs and 25 RF-84Fs (52-7254/7278), respectively. This was far below the number of aircraft SAC originally had in mind – 30 RB-36s and 75 RF-84s – but another budget crunch had arrived. The

Even the camera film magazine could be replenished while the GRF-84K was tucked in the GRB-36D's bomb bay. (U.S. Air Force)

first GRB-36D-III carrier was delivered in February 1955, six months ahead of the first GRF-84K.

The parasite could be picked up in midair enroute to the target area, or by ground hook-up prior to takeoff. Night operations were also possible. In a typical mission, the GRF-84K was carried out to a 2,810-mile radius and launched at an altitude of 25,000 feet. After completing the mission, the fighter would be recovered by the GRB-36D and returned to base. The parasite plane would be released about 800-1,000 miles from the target and within a relatively safe area. The pilot of the RF-84 would continue on to the target, obtain high- or low-level photography, as desired, then return to the carrier.

The GRB-36Ds were modified with plug-and-clearance doors instead of bomb bay doors, the FICON trapeze, a trapeze operator's station in the camera compartment, and two independent hydraulic systems for trapeze and door actuation. The clearance doors fit tight,y around the parasite during flight, while the plug doors filled the hole that remained when the GRF-84K was not being carried. Special night and rendezvous lighting was installed

When the F-84 was in the bomb bay, space was at a premium. Nevertheless, the pilot of the fighter could get out of the aircraft with some assistance. Note the handholds on the bottom of the wing carry-through structure. This is the YF-84 inside the JRB-36F, evidenced by the fixed nose hook on the fighter. Production bombers were very similar however. (Lockheed Martin)

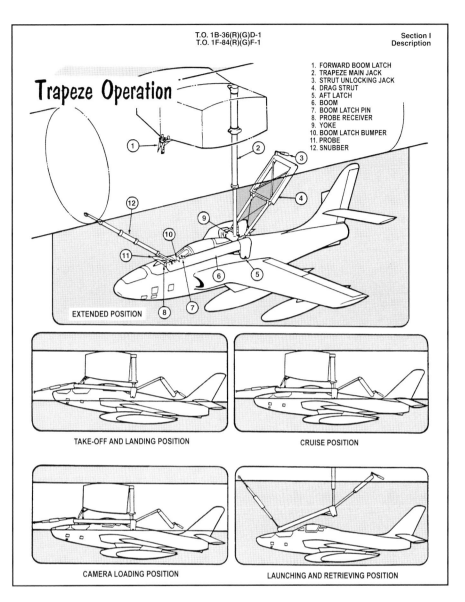

T.O. 1B-36(R)(G)D-1
T.O. 1F-84(R)(G)F-1

Section I
Description

Trapeze Operation

1. FORWARD BOOM LATCH
2. TRAPEZE MAIN JACK
3. STRUT UNLOCKING JACK
4. DRAG STRUT
5. AFT LATCH
6. BOOM
7. BOOM LATCH PIN
8. PROBE RECEIVER
9. YOKE
10. BOOM LATCH BUMPER
11. PROBE
12. SNUBBER

EXTENDED POSITION

TAKE-OFF AND LANDING POSITION

CRUISE POSITION

CAMERA LOADING POSITION

LAUNCHING AND RETRIEVING POSITION

Project Tom-Tom was a different approach to carrying fighters. Special mechanisms on the wingtips locked together and the fighters were towed along with their engines off. This method allowed the B-36 to carry two RF-84Fs, but did not allow the fighter pilots the chance to get out of their aircraft for the long trip, or for the bomber to rearm the fighters like FICON. However, the fighters could shut down their engines, and there was even consideration given to offloading the fighter fuel onto the carrier to reduce the wing loading of the fighters while they were carried. (Peter M. Bowers Collection)

A topside view of the docking mechanism during a ground test where the F-84 and B-36 were mated using overhead derricks. In this photo the F-84 has just made initial contact with the B-36 docking arm. The docking arm would be retracted into the fairing, and the wingtip of the F-84 secured at the trailing edge using a locking mechanism, shown at right in a bottom view of the same test. (Lockheed Martin)

on the GRB-36D horizontal stabilizers and under the fuselage, and an APX-29A IFF/rendezvous set was installed. The bomb bay was equipped with a catwalk, safety wires, and handholds so that the GRF-84K pilot could ingress/egress during flight. Since the B-36 did not normally carry jet fuel (the jet engines were modified to run on aviation gas), an 1,140-gallon fuel tank filled with JP-4 was carried off-

set to the left side (to clear the GRF-84K's tail) in bomb bay No. 4 so that the GRF-84K could be refueled while mated.[2] The GRB-36D could also supply electrical power, preheat air, and pressurization air to the parasite during flight.

The GRB-36D carriers saw limited service with the 99th Strategic Reconnaissance Wing based at Fairchild AFB, operating in a team

with GRF-84Ks of the 91st Strategic Reconnaissance Squadron based at nearby Larson AFB. No details have been released concerning the missions flown by the FICONs, but stories have circulated that the RF-84Ks made several overflights of the Soviet Union on reconnaissance missions prior to the U-2 becoming available. Once the U-2 had proven its capability, the FICONs were quickly phased out of service.

TOM-TOM

Several other bizarre experiments were performed during the late 1940s and early 1950s to test the feasibility of extending the range of jet fighters by having them carried into the combat zone by bombers. None of these range-extension experiments was more bizarre than Projects TIP TOW and Tom-Tom where jet fighters were attached to the wingtips of B-29s and B-36s.

Two F-84Ds (48-641 and 48-661) were modified for the initial TIP TOW tests under the designation EF-84D. The wingtips of the EF-84Ds were modified so that they could be attached to flexible mounts fitted to the wingtips of a specially modified EB-29A (44-62093).

This idea proved to be highly dangerous, although several successful linkups were made. Tragically, midway through the planned test series, the entire three-plane B-29 array crashed as a unit on 24 April 1953, killing everybody on all three aircraft. TIP TOW was cancelled.

A parallel project was undertaken with a pair of RF-84Fs (51-1848 and 51-1849) attached to wingtip hookup assemblies on the initial JRB-36F testbed (49-2707). After the TIP TOW crash, flight tests continued for a few months with this three-plane array. Only a few hookup attempts were made, and wingtip vortices and turbulence made this operation a very dangerous affair. One RF-84F was actually torn free from the bomber's wing during a linkup. The project was abandoned in late 1953, since experiments with mid-air refueling techniques seemed to offer greater promise for increased fighter ranges with far less risk to the lives of aircrews.

YB-60

It was clear early-on that the B-36 replacement was going to be the Boeing B-52, although at the beginning it was not nearly as clear if the B-52 was going to be a turboprop or a pure-jet aircraft. By January 1951 the first two B-52s were being assembled and the general configuration of the eight-engine jet bomber was well known. Although the Air Force never conducted an actual competition for possible B-52 alternatives, both Convair and Douglas worked on various designs that could fill the role.

The Douglas design that was most promising was the 1211-J turboprop revealed in January 1951. The design was for a swept-wing aircraft with a design gross weight of 322,000 pounds, a speed of 450 knots at 55,000 feet, and an absolute range of 11,000 miles. The design looked similar to the Soviet Tu-4 Bear bomber.[3]

Convair also wrestled with the question of pure-jet versus turboprop propulsion. At one point the Convair options included a six-turboprop design that had each engine housed in its own pod slung beneath the wings, and a pure-jet version that used 12 J47 engines in six pods beneath the wings.[4]

On 25 August 1950, Convair submitted an unsolicited proposal for an all-jet swept-winged version of the B-36. The Air Force was sufficiently interested that on 15 March 1951 they authorized (contract No. AF-33(038)-2182) Convair to convert two uncompleted B-36Fs (49-2676 and 49-2684) into B-36Gs. Since the aircraft was so radically different from the existing B-36, the designation was soon changed to YB-60. By the 20 August 1951 mockup review, it was noted that the turbojet engines were scheduled to be replaced by turboprop engines in June 1953. Production of either aircraft configuration, could begin in March 1953 if authorization was received by 1 January 1952.[5]

In the interest of economy, as many components as possible of the existing B-36F were used to build the YB-60. The fuselage from aft of the

The YB-60s were built in the Hangar Building, not on the main assembly line. The engines were the pacing item in the YB-60s development, and the late delivery of the J57s delayed the aircraft's first flight. (Lockheed Martin)

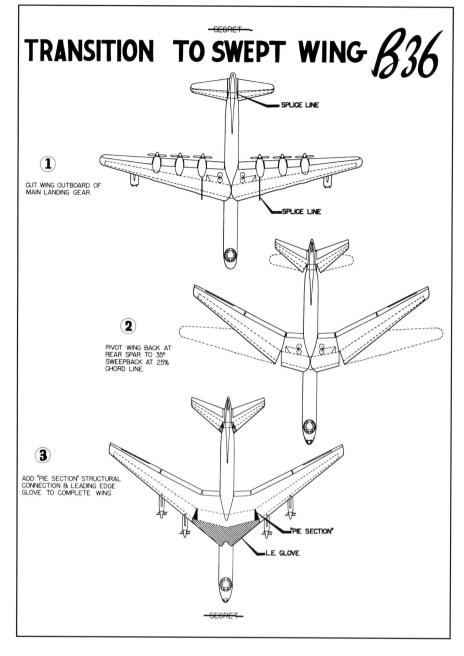

TRANSITION TO SWEPT WING *B36*

① CUT WING OUTBOARD OF MAIN LANDING GEAR.

SPLICE LINE

SPLICE LINE

② PIVOT WING BACK AT REAR SPAR TO 35° SWEEPBACK AT 25% CHORD LINE.

③ ADD "PIE SECTION" STRUCTURAL CONNECTION & LEADING EDGE GLOVE TO COMPLETE WING.

"PIE SECTION"

L.E. GLOVE

How to convert a B-36 to a swept wing in three easy steps. The majority of the structural pieces (spars, etc.) were shared between the B-36 and YB-60. (Convair via the San Diego Aerospace Museum)

to continue the sweep line to the fuselage. The net result was a wing area to 5,239 square feet, an increase of almost 500 square feet. The wing span was 206 feet, about 24 feet less than that of the B-36F. An entirely new leading and trailing edge was fabricated, including new flaps and ailerons. The aircraft was also fitted with swept vertical and horizontal stabilizers, making the aircraft slightly taller than the B-36F. Most of the structure inside the new horizontal and vertical surfaces were common with the B-36, simply angled appropriately, covered with new skin, and fitted with new control surfaces. Eight 8,700 pounds-thrust Pratt & Whitney J57-P-3 turbojets were housed in four pairs suspended below and forward of the wing leading edge, similar to the B-52.

The first YB-60 had only five crew members – pilot, copilot, navigator, bombardier/radio operator, and radio operator/tail gunner – all seated in the pressurized forward compartment. All of the defensive armament was eliminated except the tail turret, which was remotely directed by an APG-32 radar. The K-3A bombing/navigation system, with its associated Y-3A bomb sight, was retained. The maximum bomb load capacity of 86,000 pounds was the same as the B-36F.

The second prototype and production aircraft would have carried a crew of nine. The pilot, copilot-engineer, bombardier, navigator-gunner, engineer-gunner were in the forward compartment, and a radio-ECM operation, tail gunner, and two gunners were in a pressurized aft compartment. The copilot's seat tracks were arranged such that he could move his entire seat to the engineer's panel if necessary during flight. The two lower aft sighting stations were

cabin to near the end of the tail remained essentially the same as that of the B-36F. However, the nose was lengthened to accommodate more equipment, and was tapered to a needle-like instrument probe. The aft fuselage was modified to house a braking parachute and a retractable tail wheel to protect the tail section against nose-high landings. At 171

feet, the fuselage was almost nine feet longer than that of the B-36F.

A wing sweep of 37° was accomplished by cutting each main wing spar outboard of the main landing gear, and inserting a wedge-shaped structure at each location to angle the main spar 35°. A glove was added to the leading edge of the center wing

positioned higher on the fuselage to improve crew comfort during use. Interestingly, the tunnel that B-36 crewmembers could use to move between the two compartments was deleted because "… the arrangement of equipment and functions of crew members make it unnecessary." Galleys, bunks, and lavatory facilities were installed in each compartment. Production aircraft were to include two upper forward turrets and two lower aft turrets, with standard B-36 optical sights located in four sighting blisters (two forward and two aft). The tail gun-laying radar would switch to the APG-41 scheduled for use on the B-36H, and a modified APG-41 would be incorporated in the nose to control the two upper forward turrets, in addition to "… furnishing information to the pilot for evasive maneuver tactics." The normal APR-4, APR-9, and ALA-2 ECM equipment would have been replaced with an APR-14, and an APT-16 added. Convair also proposed using a new type of turret that retracted flush with the upper surface of the aircraft, eliminating the doors found on the B-36. This would simplify maintenance, and decrease the time necessary to deploy the turrets when necessary.[6]

Production B-60s would have mounted the K-3A's APS-23 search radar behind a flush radome in the nose. The packaging arrangement for the entire K-3A system was unique. All the components, including the antenna and radome, were installed on a pallet that could easily be removed from the aircraft for maintenance. This arrangement also eliminated a variety of connectors and interconnecting cables which, it was hoped, would eliminate several areas that had proven troublesome in the B-36 installation. The entire K-3A pallet would be pressurized,

and accessible by the crew during flight for maintenance. The designers were not terribly confident that this arrangement would improve the reliability of the K-3A, and they built in a complete set of test equipment and oscilloscopes on the pallet. Ten fuel tanks in the wings held 42,106 gallons of fuel. A little behind the times – the Boeing-designed flying boom was becoming operational by then – Convair included a probe-and-drogue refueling system in the production specification.[7]

The conversion of the first aircraft (49-2676) began in the spring of 1951 in the Hanger Building at Fort Worth (not in the main production building). The work was completed in only eight months, since almost 72% of the parts were identical to the B-36F. However, the project was delayed by the late delivery of the J57 turbojets, which did not arrive at Convair until April 1952. The aircraft was rolled out on 6 April 1952, and was the largest jet aircraft in the world at the time.

The YB-60 made its maiden flight on 18 April 1952, with Convair chief test

pilot Beryl A. Erikson at the controls. The Boeing YB-52 took to the air for the first time only three days later. Although there was never any formal competition between the YB-60 and the YB-52, the B-52 quickly exhibited a clear superiority. The YB-60 had a cost advantage over the B-52 because of its commonality with the B-36, but the B-52 clearly had a superior performance. The top speed of the YB-60 was only 508 mph at 39,250 feet, more than 100 mph slower than the B-52. In addition, flight tests of the YB-60 turned up a number of deficiencies, including engine surge, control system buffeting, rudder flutter, and electrical system problems. The stability was rather poor because of the high aerodynamic forces on the control surfaces acting in concert with fairly low aileron effectiveness. The refined aerodynamics of the B-52, which had been designed from the beginning as a high-speed aircraft, quickly proved their worth.

Consequently, the Air Force concluded that there was no future for the YB-60, and cancelled the flight test program on 20 January 1953 after accumulating only 66 flight hours.

A good photo of the first YB-60 with the tail wheel deployed. The swept wing greatly upset the center of gravity at high gross weights, necessitating the tail wheel during taxi. The wheel was retracted during take off after sufficient speed was attained to allow the elevators to be effective, but before rotation. After landing, the wheel was lowered after the roll-out was complete. (Lockheed Martin)

The second prototype under construction. Note that the fuselage says "B-60," not YB-60. The detachable nose section is in the lower left corner of the photo with the front radome swung open to allow access to the electronics. Note the deployed upper gun turrets – confirming that production B-60s would have been equipped with guns. (Lockheed Martin)

The second B-60 prototype featured the production-style detachable nose with the search radar mounted behind the lower flush radome and an APG-41 fire control radar in the very front. Unfortunately, this aircraft never flew before the program was cancelled. (Lockheed Martin)

The second prototype was never flown, although it was 95% complete, basically only missing its engines.

Following the brief flight test program by the first aircraft, the two YB-60s were shunted off to the side of the runway at Fort Worth, where they sat out in the weather for several months. The Air Force formally accepted the aircraft on 1 July 1954 after decided that it was costing too much to maintain the aircraft. The same day workmen took axes and blow torches to the aircraft. By the end of July, they had both been scrapped, with some of the components that were common with the B-36F being scavenged for spare parts. The cost of the YB-60 program was approximately $15 million.[8]

Convair also considered trying to adapt the YB-60 as a commercial jet airliner, again to no avail. A proposal for a 380,000 pound gross weight commercial version was powered by eight P&W J57-P-1 engines, and carried 261 passengers, a flight crew of five, and a cabin crew of four. It was expected the aircraft would cost $7 million, plus an additional $1 million for engines. The aircraft would have had a maximum range of 3,450 miles, and would have been available in December 1956. Interestingly, although the aircraft could fly nonstop from New York to London with 261 passengers, it could only carry 22 passengers on the return flight because of the prevailing 100 mph east wind encountered at cruising altitude.[9]

As part of this proposal, Convair surveyed a variety of commercial airports to determine if they could handle aircraft of this size. None of the three major airports (Los Angles, Chicago Midway, or New York Idlewild) could accommodate

The NB-36H can lay claim to be the only U.S. aircraft to carry an operating nuclear reactor airborne. The reactor did not provide any power to the aircraft, but allowed engineers to gather "real world" data on the operation of reactors and their shielding aboard aircraft. (Lockheed Martin)

an aircraft with the proposed wingspan or gross weight. Convair estimated that operating costs could be covered with an average of 215 passengers per flight. But engineers also noted that the YB-60 derivative only had a projected speed of 432 mph, compared with 550 mph for the Boeing 707 and other competitors. In the end, Convair decided to concentrate on the 880-series of jet transports instead.

ATOMIC AIRCRAFT

Interest in atomic energy hit full force following World War II. The scientists who had raced to produce a bomb had also developed a number of other possible uses for the atom. Ideas ranged from power generation to nuclear excavation to nuclear propulsion for vehicles on land, sea, and in the air. There were proposals for atomic-powered ships, submarines, locomotives, automobiles, and aircraft.

In May 1946 the Air Force initiated the Nuclear Energy for the Propulsion of Aircraft (NEPA) project to support developing long-range strategic bombers and other high-performance aircraft. Nuclear power showed promise in both fields because of its dual nature of almost unlimited fuel and the high temperatures theoretically possible using a reactor. The NEPA contract was awarded to the Fairchild Engine & Airframe Co., and the work was conducted at Oak Ridge. By the end of 1948 the Air Force had invested approximately $10 million in the program, and studies continued until 1951.

The NEPA project was replaced by the Aircraft Nuclear Propulsion (ANP) program, a joint effort between the Atomic Energy Commission (AEC) and the Air Force to develop a full-scale aircraft reactor and engine system. One of the factors that led to the ANP program was a

1948 MIT study that concluded that "… nuclear aircraft (manned) were likely less difficult than nuclear ramjets, which, in turn, would be less difficult than nuclear rockets to develop." Ironically, this turned out to be the opposite of what would later be found. Although nuclear ramjets, under Project Pluto, and nuclear rockets, under Project Rover, were successfully tested at the levels needed for operational use, an operational-level atomic aircraft powerplant was never developed.

NB-36H

The ANP program did spawn plans for two flight vehicles. The first was an effort to more fully understand the shielding requirements for an airborne reactor. A decision was made to build a small reactor and flight test it aboard a B-36. The reactor would not provide any power to the aircraft, but would be operated in flight and both the reactor and its associated radiation levels would be carefully monitored during a series of flight tests. This aircraft was referred to as the Nuclear Test Aircraft (NTA), and its development was carried out under contract AF33(038)-21117, while construction of the Nuclear Aircraft Research Facility at Fort Worth to support the program was accomplished under contract AF33(600)-6216.[10]

Convair spent a surprising amount of time defining the crew compartment for the NB-36H and its five crewmembers. The preliminary design for an appropriate crew compartment exceeded the structural limitations of the B-36H forward fuselage by a rather large margin and was rejected. A decision on 4 June 1952 to delete some crew comfort items and to move some equipment to other locations on the aircraft, resulted in weight estimates within the structural limitations of the aircraft. After evaluating seven alternatives, the final

design had a pilot and copilot at stations essentially similar to the standard B-36, although lower in the fuselage. Two nuclear engineers were located immediately aft of the pilots, facing forward. The flight engineer was located in the extreme necked-down aft end of the compartment on the centerline of the airplane, also facing forward.

Construction of a crew compartment mockup began in July 1952. The new nose section would replace the conventional nose section on the B-36H forward of station 5. The basic fuselage lines of the aircraft would remain substantially the same, except the new crew compartment was slightly shorter. Also, the nose landing gear would be moved six inches forward to accommodate the entry hatch to the crew compartment.

Although the B-36 was a large aircraft, and the normal crew compartment provided a great deal of room for the crew, the NB-36H would not

have this luxury. The shielding required to protect the crew greatly decreased the space available. The station arrangements were carefully planned to obtain the maximum efficiency from the crew and their equipment within the confined area of the compartment. For example, one problem concerned the placement of the nuclear engineer's oxygen regulators and interphone panels. It was finally decided that the instruments could be mounted on a drop-door hinged to the base of each nuclear engineer's seat. When let down, the door fell between the engineer's legs just above his feet, allowing him to see the instruments. When not in use, the door was pushed upright against the seat, out of the way.

At the pilot's stations, there was only a single set of instruments, located in the middle of the panel since there was not sufficient room behind the panel for all the normal plumbing and electrical wiring. The engine scanning normally performed by

The NB-36H crew compartment and reactor vessel on stands in the nuclear area at Fort Worth. Both were radioactive and sent to Mountain Ridge for permanent storage. Note the fancy "keep out" sign in the foreground. (Lockheed Martin)

The shielded crew compartment being removed from the NB-36H after the completion of the flight test program. The compartment was designed to be removed intact. (Lockheed Martin)

crewmembers in the aft compartment was performed instead by using television cameras. A location for the television itself could not be found, however, until it was decided to locate it in the overhead area between the two nuclear engineers, where it could be seen relatively easily by the flight engineer.

Although the two pilots had movable seats, the other three seats were fixed to the structure. The area under the seats was used for storage.

A drinking water container was provided in the aft portion of the copilot's seat, while the aft side of the pilot's seat contained a relief tube. This location was chosen since it allowed crewmembers to stand at the only location in the compartment that was full-height. A conventional toilet was located outside the crew compartment in the fuselage near the entrance hatch.

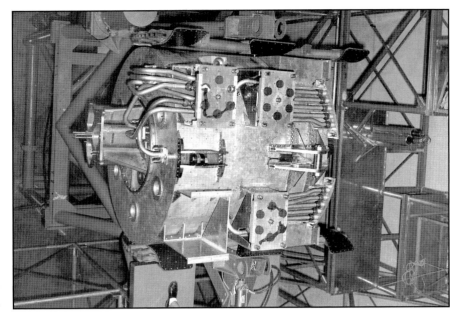

The ASTR reactor before it was loaded into the NB-36H. The view is looking down at the reactor from the top of its loading pit. (Lockheed Martin)

The yellow glass used in the windshield to provide shielding for the crew made the conventional gray color normally used in cockpits turn a very undesirable color. After much experimenting, designers found that using a lavender paint in the pilots' area gave the illusion of being gray when illuminated by daylight through the yellow windshield. The pilots' instrument panel was painted black, but all other panels were painted a very pale gray that made the compartment appear roomier. The seats were upholstered in light gray cloth, and the floors were covered in darker gray carpet. A curtain was installed between the pilots and the nuclear engineers to block sunlight.[11]

All portions of the exterior seen from the pilots' compartment were painted flat black to minimize glare. The initial design of a simple antiglare shield produced an unattractive pattern when combined with the black radome. The two areas were subsequently blended together and a small amount of trim extended upward and aft to provide a more appealing look.

Since the crew compartment was designed to be removable during

The B-36H that was selected for use as the NB-36H had been damaged in the tornado that hit Carswell AFB on 1 September 1952. Damage was mostly limited to this gash on the left side of the forward fuselage, and to the entire right side of the cockpit being caved in from an impact with another aircraft. Convair estimated that the entire fuselage forward of the wing needed replaced, making this a logical choice for conversion to the nuclear test aircraft. (via Don Pyeatt)

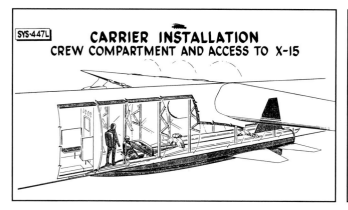

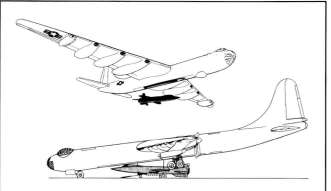

When the X-15 research airplane program first began, it was expected that a B-36 would be used as a carrier aircraft. The X-15 would be carried suspended in the B-36 bomb bays, much the same as earlier X-planes had been carried by B-29s. The pilot could ingress/egress the X-15 during flight, something not possible with the final B-52 solution, although the B-52 offered much higher performance. Note the early tall vertical stabilizer on the X-15. (left: Johnny Armstrong Collection via Frederick A. Johnsen; right: National Advisory Committee on Aeronautics)

maintenance, a method had to be devised to easily connect and disconnect the flight controls. Instead of the normal cables, a series of push-pull rods projecting from the bottom of the crew compartment was devised that could easily be connected to the cables in the lower fuselage. Push-pull rods were also used for both the pilots' and flight engineer's throttle and mixture controls. These rods connected to the normal cable underneath the crew compartment.

The NTA began its life as a B-36H (51-5712) that had been extensively damaged during a tornado at Carswell AFB on 1 September 1952. Since a new shielded crew compartment was part of the plan for the NTA, this airframe was a logical choice. The aircraft was redesignated XB-36H on 11 March 1955, and was again redesignated as NB-36H on 6 June 1955. The name *Convair Crusader* was painted on each side of the forward fuselage during a portion of the flight test series.

The NB-36H was modified to carry a small air-cooled reactor in the aft bomb bay and to provide shielding for the crew. The NTA incorporated shielding around the reactor itself and a totally new nose section which housed a twelve-ton lead and rubber shielded compartment for the crew. There were also water jackets in the fuselage and behind the crew compartment to absorb radiation. The crew was housed entirely in a modified compartment in the fuselage nose section. The compartment was composed of lead and rubber, and entirely surrounded the crew. A four-ton lead disc shield was installed in the middle of the aircraft. Only the pilot and copilot could see out through the foot-thick, leaded-glass windshield. A closed-circuit television system enabled the crew to watch the reactor.

The 1,000-kilowatt ASTR reactor that weighed 35,000 pounds was installed in a container that could be carried in bomb bay No. 4. The reac-

tor could be removed from the aircraft while on the ground. The reactor was made critical in flight on several occasions and the aircraft was used for many radiation and shielding experiments. Its first flight was made on 17 September 1955, with test pilot A.S. Witchell, Jr. at the controls. Flying alongside the NB-36H on every flight was a C-97 carrying a platoon of armed Marines ready to parachute down and surround the test aircraft in case it crashed. A total of 47 flights were made through March 1957. The NB-36H was decommissioned at Fort Worth in late 1957 and scrapped several months later, with the radioactive parts being buried.

The flight program showed that the "aircraft normally would pose no threat, even if flying low." The principal concerns were accidents which cause the release of fission products from the reactors, and the dosage from exposure to leaked radioactivity (in the direct cycle concept).

[1] Aircraft History Cards supplied by Mike Moore, Lockheed Martin, Fort Worth. [2] 1B-36(R)D(G)-1 FICON Flight Manual, 17 June 1955. [3] Aviation Week, 29 January 1951, p 13. [4] Ibid. [5] *Mockup Inspection of the Model YB-60 Airplane*, Convair, Contract No. AF-33(038)-2182, 20 August 1951, p 3. [6] Ibid, p 11. This represented the inclusion of MCRs 5009-5012, 5014-5016, and 5020-5022. [7] Ibid, p 22. [8] Fort Worth Star, various dates in July 1954. [9] Convair report FZP-36-1001, *YB-60 Commercial Transport*, 4 April 1953. [10] Convair report XM-566, *Short History of the Design and Development of the Nose Section and Crew Compartment Mock-Up for the XB-36H*, 20 March 1956. [11] Ibid.

B-36, XC-99, AND YB-60 SERIAL NUMBERS

DESIGNATION	SERIAL NUMBER(S)	QUANTITY	CONTRACT NUMBER	NOTES
XB-36-CF	42-13570	1	W535-ac-22352	
YB-36-CF	42-13571	1	W535-ac-22352	To RB-36E
XC-99-1-CO	43-52436	1	W535-ac-34454	On display at the former Kelly AFB
B-36A-1-CF	44-92004/92006	3	AF33-038-AC7	To RB-36E (except 44-92004, Static Test Article)
B-36A-5-CF	44-92007/92011	5	AF33-038-AC7	To RB-36E
B-36A-10-CF	44-92012/92017	6	AF33-038-AC7	To RB-36E
B-36A-15-CF	44-92018/92025	8	AF33-038-AC7	To RB-36E
B-36B-1-CF	44-92026/92037	12	AF33-038-AC7	To B-36D
B-36B-5-CF	44-92038/92049	12	AF33-038-AC7	To B-36D
B-36B-10-CF	44-92050/92064	15	AF33-038-AC7	To B-36D (92057 was jet prototype)
B-36B-15-CF	44-92065/92079	15	AF33-038-AC7	To B-36D except 92075 and 92079 (crashed)
B-36B-20-CF	44-92080/92087	8	AF33-038-AC7	To B-36D
B-36D-1-CF	44-92095/92098	4	AF33-038-AC7	Ordered as B-36B
B-36	44-92099/92103	5	AF33-038-AC7	Cancelled
B-36D-5-CF	49-2647/2654	8	AF33-039-2182	
B-36D-35-CF	49-2655	1	AF33-039-2182	Last B-36D delivered
B-36D-15-CF	49-2656/2657	2	AF33-039-2182	
B-36D-25-CF	49-2658/2663	6	AF33-039-2182	
B-36D-35-CF	49-2664/2668	5	AF33-039-2182	
RB-36D-1-CF	44-92088/92094	7	AF33-038-AC7	Ordered as B-36B
RB-36D-5-CF	49-2686	1	AF33-039-2182	
RB-36D-10-CF	49-2687/2693	7	AF33-039-2182	
RB-36D-15-CF	49-2694/2697	4	AF33-039-2182	
RB-36D-20-CF	49-2698/2702	5	AF33-039-2182	
B-36F-1-CF	49-2669/2675	7	AF33-039-2182	
B-36F-1-CF	49-2677	1	AF33-039-2182	
B-36F-5-CF	49-2678/2683	6	AF33-039-2182	
B-36F-5-CF	49-2685	1	AF33-039-2182	
B-36F-10-CF	50-1064/1073	10	AF33-039-2182	
B-36F-15-CF	50-1074/1082	9	AF33-039-2182	
RB-36F-1-CF	49-2703/2711	9	AF33-039-2182	
RB-36F-5-CF	49-2712/2721	10	AF33-039-2182	
RB-36F-10-CF	50-1098/1099	2	AF33-039-2182	
RB-36F-15-CF	50-1100/1102	3	AF33-039-2182	
YB-60-1-CF	49-2676	1	AF33-039-2182	Ordered as B-36F-1-CF
YB-60-2-CF	49-2684	1	AF33-039-2182	Ordered as B-36F-5-CF
B-36H-1-CF	50-1083/1091	9	AF33-039-2182	
B-36H-5-CF	50-1092/1097	6	AF33-039-2182	
B-36H-10-CF	51-5699/5705	7	AF33-039-2182	
B-36H-15-CF	51-5706/5711	6	AF33-039-2182	
B-36H-20-CF	51-5712/5717	6	AF33-039-2182	
B-36H-25-CF	51-5718/5723	6	AF33-039-2182	
B-36H-30-CF	51-5724/5729	6	AF33-039-2182	
B-36H-35-CF	51-5730/5735	6	AF33-039-2182	
B-36H-40-CF	51-5736/5742	7	AF33-039-2182	
B-36H-45-CF	52-1343/1347	5	AF33-038-5793	
B-36H-50-CF	52-1348/1353	6	AF33-038-5793	
B-36H-55-CF	52-1354/1359	6	AF33-038-5793	
B-36H-60-CF	52-1360/1366	7	AF33-038-5793	
RB-36H-1-CF	50-1103/1105	3	AF33-039-2182	
RB-36H-5-CF	50-1106/1110	5	AF33-039-2182	
RB-36H-10-CF	51-5743/5747	5	AF33-039-2182	
RB-36H-15-CF	51-5748/5753	6	AF33-039-2182	
RB-36H-20-CF	51-5754/5756	3	AF33-039-2182	
RB-36H-20-CF	51-13717/13719	3	AF33-039-2182	
RB-36H-25-CF	51-13720/13725	6	AF33-039-2182	
RB-36H-30-CF	51-13726/13731	6	AF33-039-2182	51-13730 on display at Castle AFB
RB-36H-35-CF	51-13732/13737	6	AF33-039-2182	
RB-36H-40-CF	51-13738/13741	4	AF33-039-2182	
RB-36H-45-CF	52-1367/1373	7	AF33-038-5793	
RB-36H-50-CF	52-1374/1380	7	AF33-038-5793	
RB-36H-55-CF	52-1381/1386	6	AF33-038-5793	
RB-36H-60-CF	52-1387/1392	6	AF33-038-5793	
B-36J-1-CF	52-2210/2221	12	AF33-038-5793	52-2217 on display at SAC Museum; 52-2220 on display at U.S. Air Force Museum
B-36J-5-CF	52-2222/2818	12	AF33-038-5793	
B-36J-10-CF	52-2819/2827	9	AF33-038-5793	52-2827 undergoing restoration at Fort Worth

SIGNIFICANT MODIFICATIONS:

YB-36A – Structural Test Article

B-36A   44-92004

GRB-36D-III – FICON Carrier Aircraft

RB-36D-1-CF	44-92090
RB-36D-1-CF	44-92092
RB-36D-1-CF	44-92094
RB-36D-10-CF	49-2687
RB-36D-10-CF	49-2692
RB-36D-15-CF	49-2694
RB-36D-15-CF	49-2695
RB-36D-15-CF	49-2696
RB-36D-20-CF	49-2701
RB-36D-20-CF	49-2702

JRB-36F – FICON and Tom-Tom Test Aircraft

RB-36F-1-CF   49-2707
Sometimes listed a GRB-36F

NB-36H – Nuclear Test Aircraft
B-36H-20-CF   51-5712
Originally B-36H. XB-36H on 11 March 1955. NB-36H on 6 June 1955.

DB-36H – RASCAL Missile Launch Aircraft
B-36H-1-CF   50-1085
Originally B-36H. DB-36H in July 1955.

B-36H-15-CF   51-5706
Originally B-36H. DB-36H in January 1955. JDB-36H in February 1955. EDB-36H in August 1955. JDB-36H in November 1955.

B-36H-15-CF   51-5710
Originally B-36H. EDB-36H in September 1952. JDB-36H in November 1955.

B-36H – TANBO XIV Refueling Tests

B-36H-15-CF   51-5706
Originally B-36H. DB-36H in January 1955. JDB-36H in February 1955. EDB-36H in August 1955. JDB-36H in November 1955.

RESTORATION

Restoration Director Bill Plumlee discussing a plan for the last remaining R-4360 engine from the Fort Worth B-36J. At one point in the 1970s, attempts had been made to fly the B-36J and major work had been accomplished on the engines. (Aviation Heritage Association via Don Pyeatt)

Front fuselage and main wing section following the separation of the aft fuselage. Although in need of major work, partially because of vandalism, the aircraft was remarkably complete externally. The B-36J had been completed on the assembly line as a Featherweight III aircraft and had not been equipped with defensive armament except the tail turret. (Aviation Heritage Association via Don Pyeatt)

The large rudder being removed from the vertical stabilizer. Note the empty holes for the tail turret and twin antenna units for the APG-41 gun laying radar.
(Aviation Heritage Association via Don Pyeatt)

Looking like new, the forward fuselage returns from Lockheed's paint shop. Many local companies have assisted with the restoration, including Lockheed Martin which purchased the Convair Division from General Dynamics in 1993. When the restoration is completed this B-36J will rival the aircraft in the Air Force Museum in appearance, a fitting tribute to the last B-36.
(Aviation Heritage Association via Don Pyeatt)

The Fort Worth B-36 has become a lifetime cause for many former Convair and SAC personnel who built and flew the Peacemakers. One person in particular, Mr. C.E. (Ed) Calvert deserves special mention for devoting his life to the preservation of this aircraft. Mr. Calvert has volunteered as a caretaker of 52-2827 since the aircraft was retired from SAC in 1959 and continues to do so as this book goes to print. After learning of Mr. Calvert's dedication to his cause, ProWeb Fort Worth, a Fort Worth based web publisher, has published an E-book on Compact Disk that details the post-service history of this aircraft and the many obstacles it has met while waiting to be placed on permanent public display. *B-36: Saving the Last Peacemaker* (ISBN 0-9677593-0-7), co-authored by Ed Calvert, Don Pyeatt, and Richard Marmo, describes the plight of the aircraft and those who undertook the monumental task of saving it from total destruction. The book is available online from Amazon.com and from the publisher's website http://www.prowebfortworth.com.

SIGNIFICANT DATES

September 1939
Hitler conquers Poland in 20 days.

11 April 1941
Requests issued to Consolidated and Boeing for preliminary studies of an intercontinental bomber.

3 May 1941
Consolidated submits preliminary data on the Model 35.

15 November 1941
The Army Air Forces orders two XB-36s (W535-ac-22352).

20 July 1942
XB-36 mockup reviewed.

17 March 1943
Consolidated Aircraft merges with Vultee Aircraft, becoming Consolidated Vultee Aircraft (Convair).

23 July 1943
A letter of intent is issued for 100 production B-36s.

25 May 1945
The Army Air Forces cancels 17,000 aircraft – but not the B-36.

8 September 1945
The first XB-36 is rolled out.

8 August 1946
The XB-36 makes its first flight.

21 March 1946
The Strategic Air Command (SAC) is established by the Army Air Forces.

18 September 1947
The U.S. Air Force is established as a separate service.

31 December 1942
A single XC-99 is ordered.

February 1945
Pan Am orders 15 Model 37 commercial versions of the XC-99.

24 January 1949
The XC-99 makes its first flight.

30 June 1948
A B-36A drops 72,000 pounds of bombs during a test flight. It's the heaviest bomb load yet carried by any bomber.

March 1949
A B-36B flies 9,600 miles in 43 hours and 37 minutes.

26 March 1949
The first jet-augmented B-36D makes its first flight.

23 April 1949
Secretary of Defense Johnson cancels the USS *United States*, sparking almost open warfare between the Navy and Air Force over the fate of the B-36.

14 January 1951
An RB-36D makes the longest known B-36 flight – 51.5 hours – without refueling.

8 January 1952
FICON flight tests with a JRB-36F and F-84E begin.

14 August 1954
The last B-36J, a Featherweight III, is delivered to the Air Force.

12 February 1959
The last B-36 is retired and SAC becomes an all-jet force.

Government Aircraft Plant No. 4 in Fort Worth. The Nuclear Area for the NB-36H program is at center in the foreground. The two YB-60s can be seen just west of the Nuclear Area. Note the #2 YB-60 is missing its rudder, removed to support the first aircraft. The XB-36 is at lower right in the open field. No fewer than 40 B-36s are around the factory buildings. (Lockheed Martin)